Working with the under-threes: responding to children's needs

EARLY INTERACTIONS

Working with the under-threes: responding to children's needs

Edited by
**Lesley Abbott and
Helen Moylett**

OPEN UNIVERSITY PRESS
Buckingham · Philadelphia

Open University Press
Celtic Court
22 Ballmoor
Buckingham
MK18 1XW

and
1900 Frost Road, Suite 101
Bristol, PA 19007, USA

First published 1997

A catalogue record of this book is available from the British Library

ISBN   0 335 19839 2 (pb)   0 335 19840 6 (hb)

A catalog record for this book is available from the Library of Congress

Copy-edited and typeset by The Running Head Limited, London and Cambridge
Printed in Great Britain by Biddles Ltd, Guildford and King's Lynn

To Connor, Evie and Kathleen and all the under-threes
from whom we learned so much

Contents

Contributors

Lesley Abbott is Professor of Early Childhood Education at the Manchester Metropolitan University where she leads the Early Years team. She is responsible for early years training and development at pre-service and in-service levels for teachers and other early years professionals. She has successfully introduced one of the first multi-professional degrees in the country – the BA (Hons) in Early Childhood Studies – and is involved in a range of projects designed to increase training opportunities for all early years professionals. She was a member of the Council for the Accreditation of Teacher Education (CATE), the Rumbold Committee and the steering group for the RSA Early Learning Project. She has contributed nationally and internationally to the development of early years work and is Director of the research project 'Shaping the Future – Educare for the Under Threes'. She has written a number of books on play in the early years and on training and has recently co-edited the successful *Quality Education in the Early Years*.

Helen Moylett is a Senior Lecturer in Education Studies at the Manchester Metropolitan University. She has worked in several inner-city Manchester primary schools in both early and later years settings, both as a class teacher and as an advisory teacher. She was a home–school liaison teacher for four years and continues to pursue her interest in home–school issues through her research and work with students. She is particularly interested in the ways in which practitioners can reflect upon and research their practice with a view to improving it.

Brenda Griffin is a member of the Early Years team and the Multi-professional Coordinator in the School of Education. She has developed a variety of in-service courses in response to the Children Act, bringing together a range of professionals working with young children and their families across the different sectors. She has been involved in the development of the BA (Hons) in Early Childhood Studies and works extensively with local authorities. Her previous experience has been in the management of combined nursery centres demanding a multi-professional approach. Her current research interests are centred on young children and their families and ways in which services, and the adults within them, respond to their needs. Her commitment to the rights of children, as defined by the UN Convention, is reflected in all her work.

Caroline Barratt-Pugh is a Senior Lecturer in the Department of Language Arts Education at the Edith Cowan University, Perth, Western Australia. She is particularly interested in bilingualism and early literacy in home and school settings. She has been involved in teaching and research in these areas for a number of years. Caroline started her early years career as a nursery nurse and then became a teacher in Bradford, Yorkshire. She joined the Early Years team at the Manchester Metropolitan University in 1987 and has been in Australia since 1992.

Julia Gillen (née Rabone) is a research student at the Manchester Metropolitan University registered for a PhD degree. She is investigating the linguistic behaviour of 3- and 4-year-olds with telephones; both in pretence play with toy phones and in actual two-way conversations. This is proving to be a fruitful arena for pursuing her two main research interests: the pretence play of young children as a window into both their language and sociocultural development; and discourse analysis. She is the mother of three young children, who have benefited from childminders, nurseries (private and subsidized), playgroups, crèches and toddler groups in Peckham, London and now Burnley, Lancashire, while Julia has juggled with combinations of work, study, and, most importantly, watching Daniel, Conor and Kathleen grow up!

Hilary Renowden trained as an early years teacher and worked in primary schools as a nursery teacher in Leicester and Clwyd. Her involvement as a tutor on Early Childhood diploma courses took her to Sweden and Denmark where she was strongly influenced by the philosophy underpinning early years work in Scandinavia. Restricted by the demands of recent legislation, and disillusioned by the pressure within the state system which she considered stifled both her own creativity and that of the children, she opened her own nursery in her own home in Clwyd. It gives her an excellent opportunity to put her philosophy into practice; there she successfully provides an environment, both indoors and outdoors, in which creative expression can flourish.

Ruth Holland is a qualified teacher who is co-owner/manager of a 60-place day nursery in south Manchester. She originally taught in secondary schools but for the last ten years has worked in early years. She is an accredited NVQ assessor and is studying part-time for a BA (Hons) in Early Childhood Education. She is particularly interested in play and learning and in the choices children make when they are playing.

Brenda Kyle is Principal of Charnwood Nursery which is a very special place funded by a charitable trust and the LEA. It provides support for all young children and their parents. She worked in mainstream primary before moving on to teaching hearing-impaired children. She has always had an interest in early years and, in particular, the importance of working with families (as opposed to working with children only). She took up her current post ten years ago and has been instrumental in the nursery's growth, development and influence on the lives of young children and their families

Fiona Fogarty works for the Language for Education Access Project funded by Section 11 and is based at Sparrow Hill Community School. She is coordinator for the project but also very much involved in structured play as a teaching and learning medium, particularly for bilingual children. She has had experience of working with all ages in the primary school but is now based in the Early Years Unit. She has first-hand experience of working with the under-threes as proud parent of Evie, aged 2 years 1 month, about whom she writes in her chapter.

Acknowledgements

As the series title suggests, this book is about interactions. These have taken place in a variety of contexts and with many people of very different ages. Without these interactions this book would not have been possible.

As editors our first debt of gratitude is to all the contributors who have provided a broad spectrum of experiences and perspectives on their work with the under-threes. They have allowed us to share their enthusiasm, concerns, successes and hopes – but above all, their commitment to young children.

We are grateful to all those under-threes who have allowed us to share their experiences and to eavesdrop on some of their 'early interactions'.

We are particularly indebted to the Esmée Fairbairn Charitable Trust who, with the Manchester Metropolitan University, have jointly funded the research project on which some of these chapters are based. We acknowledge their commitment to funding in this important field. We are very grateful to the administrative staff of the Research Base in the School of Education at the Manchester Metropolitan University, in particular Jean Davidson for her tireless and good humoured support, together with Trish Gladdis and Barbara Ashcroft; also to Julia Gillen for her advice, support, professionalism and dedication in helping us with the difficult and demanding task of editing all the contributions. Special thanks are also due to Mags Stopford and her family and to Jo Mathieson for allowing us to use their words and experience as childminders.

Tribute is also paid to the local authorities and centres on which we have relied, in particular, Stockport, Salford, Manchester and Rochdale LEAs; Briercliffe Nursery (Burnley), Charnwood Nursery (Stockport), Higher Downs Nursery (Trafford), Hilary's Nursery (Mold, Clwyd), Hollywood Park Nursery Centre (Stockport), Ladywell Community Nursery Centre (Salford), Mosside Children's Centre (Manchester), Old Moat Children's Centre (Manchester), Princess Christian Nursery (Manchester), Sparrow Hill Community School (Rochdale) and Family Day Care Centres in Western Australia.

Without all these people this series would never have been written.

Series introduction – why focus on the under-threes?

The Carnegie Task Force report on meeting the needs of young children (1994: 4) points to the 'critical importance of the first three years as being a crucial "starting point" on the child's educational journey'.

The series 'Early interactions' consists of two books, *Working with the Under-threes: Training and Professional Development* and *Working with the Under-threes: Responding to Children's Needs*. These two books aim to address some of the key issues surrounding the young child and the family as the first steps are taken on this all-important educational journey. They are intended to complement each other but are capable of standing alone.

Working with the Under-threes: Training and Professional Development both offers information on, and raises questions about, the kinds of training and professional development and support available to the wide range of adults who work with young children. It is written by a range of people with different experiences and perspectives on early education and care. Both trainers and practitioners share their experiences and raise questions which, it is hoped, will both challenge and encourage those with responsibility for children at this critical stage in their learning.

Working with the Under-threes: Responding to Children's Needs focuses upon ways in which researchers, parents and practitioners seek to meet the diverse needs of young children in specific ways. Important questions are raised with regard to children's rights and entitlement, and ways in which early interactions with people, environment, culture, curriculum and context help to shape the educational lives of children under 3.

The focus of both books is clearly on those adults responsible for the care and education of the youngest children in our society. Their experiences, views, roles and responsibilities are shared and examined from both theoretical and practical standpoints. Acknowledgement is made of the holistic nature of early learning, in which care and education are viewed as complementary and inseparable.

Writing an introduction to any new book inevitably makes the editors reflect on how far our original vision has been realized, and on what has emerged in the process. The 'intended outcomes', as anyone involved in course planning knows, whether at the level of a curriculum for children under 3 in the nursery, or the implementation of a new honours degree in a university, are those things which give the writers a real buzz of excitement and achievement, or a real headache, as they recognize just how much more there is to be written!

So guarding against the danger of writing a concluding rather than an introductory chapter, we outline some of the key aims in putting together this book.

The main aim, we both admit unashamedly, is a selfish one. At the time of writing we are both totally involved in the lives of children under 3. As Director of a two-year research project looking at 'Educare for the Under Threes', funded by the Esmée Fairbairn Charitable Trust and the Manchester Metropolitan University (1995–7), Lesley is working closely with the Early Years team at the university and with parents and practitioners in the UK and other European countries in the identification of key factors in the provision of quality out-of-home experiences for children under 3.

Helen is even more involved and has a very real vested interest in 'early interactions' as an initiator and responder to the needs and demands of her own lively under-three! Her experiences and those of Connor are discussed in Chapter 1 of *Working with the Under-threes: Responding to Children's Needs*, in which some very real dilemmas facing parents and professionals at this crucial stage in both adults' and children's lives are addressed.

Both of us have had many years' experience working with children of all ages and in planning and providing training and support for all the professionals responsible for them. We share a strong commitment to the principle of 'educare', i.e. that care and education are inseparable and that anyone who is responsible for young children is an 'educarer'.

Our work over many years with students training to teach young children, and our partnerships with schools and other early years establishments whose staff are on our in-service programme, working at diploma, degree or masters level, has convinced us of the importance of interdisciplinary involvement in the lives of young children.

Helen's work in the early 1980s as a home–school liaison teacher helped her to understand the difficult relationship parents often have with educational establishments. On the one hand, though they have love, commitment and a deep knowledge about their child, on the other, they may be swiftly deskilled by 'the experts'. She is convinced that if parents and educarers are to work together effectively throughout a child's educational career, they have to respect each other's roles and expertise and start communicating as soon as they meet – usually long before the age of compulsory schooling. Lesley's work with early years professionals in schools and centres convinced her long before 'official recommendations' were made that multi-professional training and teamwork were the answer to shared understanding and continuity in children's learning.

As a contributor to the Rumbold Report (DES 1990), *Start Right* (the RSA Early Learning Report) (Ball 1994) and the Report of the Early Years Training

Group (Pugh 1996), she became increasingly aware of the need for training and support for the vast number of early years educators currently working with children under 3, issues which are addressed in Chapter 1.

A number of factors influenced our decision to use the series title 'Early interactions'. The first is our belief, borne out by research (Trevarthen 1992; Selleck and Goldschmied 1996) that from birth, babies are effective initiators of early interactions.

Second, the power of early interactions in shaping future attitudes and dispositions is reinforced by research findings and our own experience. New research demonstrates young children's amazing capacity for learning in their earliest years (Trevarthen 1992; Gardner 1993; Goleman 1996); many of the chapters reflect this capacity and describe ways in which parents and educators harness and develop the skills, enthusiasm, curiosity and motivation which young children bring to every experience.

Our third reason for choosing 'Early interactions' as a series title is because this was exactly the process through which we went. As editors we engaged in early interactions in talking about why we considered a book like this was needed, what our aims were and who the contributors would be; we also realized that, because of our work in which we are in constant dialogue with a whole range of professionals, many of whom work with children under 3, we had access to a group of people with a vast range of knowledge, understanding, skill and commitment. Why not provide a much needed forum in which dialogue and interactions could begin to take place?

We are in the privileged position of having known the authors of the chapters for many years in different capacities: as colleagues within the university or local authorities in which we work, as former in-service students or ex-students, or as parents, childminders and managers of services across different sectors and departments. It was *our* 'early interactions' with these colleagues which resulted in both books.

The many issues addressed are intended to provide information and provoke further discussion. Each contributor has written from their own perspective and experience; there are still many other points of view which we have not had space to represent. Some chapters are based on research findings, particularly from the 'Educare for the Under Threes' project (Manchester Metropolitan University 1996); others reflect the day-to-day experiences of particular practitioners and the under-threes with whom they spend their time.

Key themes include the identification of, and provision for, children with special educational needs, relationships between practitioners and parents, children's rights, new training opportunities and initiatives, equality of opportunity and child protection.

It is timely, at a stage where the future of early education and care is on the political agenda, that those issues which most affect the youngest children and their educarers are acknowledged and discussed.

Issues are raised throughout concerning quality – a much defined yet still elusive concept (Abbott and Rodger 1994; Moss and Pence 1994). Questions are asked about quality interactions, care, education, training, childminding, parenting, play, programmes and support.

In the introduction to his excellent report for the Bernard Van Leer Foundation on pathways to quality, Woodhead (1996) states:

> Our perception of 'quality' in early childhood programmes can be likened to our perception of the rainbow composed as it is of sunshine and rain, it changes with every shift in perspective. And just as people have searched for the illusory crock of gold at the rainbow's end, so development experts search for universal definitions and standards of quality. But quality is contextual . . . Sensitivity to diversity and to one's own preconceptions should be key elements informing all early childhood work.

Because of the diversity of roles and experience of the writers of these chapters it is inevitable that a range of contexts and perspectives are represented. We hope that readers will recognize and welcome these diversities.

While we agree with Woodhead that 'quality is contextual' we also consider that there are certain underlying principles which should underpin any educare service, programme or interaction, irrespective of context. These are to do with the rights and entitlements of children however young they might be.

Cathy Nutbrown (1996) in the title of her book encompasses children's right to 'respectful educators' and to become 'capable learners'. She quotes the four goals for a policy on children held by the Children's Welfare Commission in Denmark (Vilien 1993):

- to respect the child as an individual in the family and in society;
- to give the child a central position in the life of grown-ups;
- to promote – in a wider sense – the physical conditions in which children grow up;
- to promote equal opportunities in the conditions of life of children, both in a material and in a cultural sense.

While we are aware that in Denmark national policy ensures that young children are valued and those who work with them are respected, surely these aims should hold for all young children in all societies and cultures.

Siraj-Blatchford (1996: 23) also emphasizes the need for 'promoting respect for all groups and individuals regardless of "difference"'. She points out that

> Despite the calm and friendly appearance that most early childcare and education settings display there may be a great deal of inequality in for instance, the interactions, displays, policies or curriculum that staff offer. These are important issues to be considered because they concern the early socialisation of both the oppressed and the oppressors. In other words, here we have a real concern for people with, and without, power to affect one another's behaviour, their actions, intentions and beliefs.

Goldschmied and Jackson (1994) talk about 'people under three', not babies, toddlers, or even children, but people with rights which include being treated with dignity and respect.

Article 2 (1) of the UN Convention on the Rights of the Child (UNICEF 1989) states:

1. The States Parties to the present Convention shall respect and ensure the rights set forth in the Convention to each child within their jurisdiction without discrimination of any kind, irrespective of the child's or his or her parents' or legal guardian's race, colour, sex, language, religion, political or other opinion, national, ethnic or social origin, property, disability, birth or other status.

2. States Parties shall take all appropriate measures to ensure that the child is protected against all forms of discrimination or punishment on the basis of the status, activities, expressed opinions, or beliefs of the child's parents, legal guardians or family members.

Throughout both books in this series the writers have focused on specific aspects of 'educare' with the intention of addressing both the needs and rights of young children. We recognize the need for children under 3 to be nurtured in a safe, supportive environment in which they are given appropriate experiences which provide them with opportunities to learn and grow. *Working with the Under-threes: Training and Professional Development* focuses on the training and professional development needs of the adults who work with under-threes in out-of-home settings. Children have the right to positive relationships with adults who will foster their self-concept and develop their self-esteem, will value their home language and provide opportunities to acquire basic literacy and oracy skills. We recognize young children's entitlement to be treated as 'special' and for their needs to be properly met in an environment which supports and fosters their growing independence. *Working with the Under-threes: Responding to Children's Needs* also relates to these entitlements but concentrates on particular adults responding to children's needs.

To the 'educarer', whether as parent, childminder, nursery officer, teacher or playgroup leader, is given the responsibility for providing the kinds of quality experiences which are instrumental in bringing about appropriate *early interactions*.

References

Abbott, L. and Rodger, R. (eds) (1994) *Quality Education in the Early Years*. Buckingham: Open University Press.

Ball, C. (1994) *Start Right: The Importance of Early Learning*. London: Royal Society for the Encouragement of the Arts, Manufacture and Commerce.

Carnegie Task Force (1994) *Starting Points – Meeting the Needs of Our Youngest Children*. New York: Carnegie Corporation.

Department of Education and Science [DES] (1990) *Starting with Quality, the Report of the Committee of Inquiry into the Quality of Educational Experience Offered to 3 and 4-year-olds*. London: HMSO.

Gardner, H. (1993) *Multiple Intelligences: The Theory in Practice*. New York: Basic Books.

Goldschmied, E. and Jackson, S. (1994) *People Under Three*. London: Routledge.

Goleman, D. (1996) *Emotional Intelligence – Why it Can Matter more than IQ*. London: Bloomsbury.

Moss, P. and Pence, A. (1994) *Valuing Quality in Early childhood Services*. London: Paul Chapman.

Nutbrown, C. (ed.) (1996) *Respectful Educators – Capable Learners, Children's Rights and Early Education*. London: Paul Chapman.

Pugh, G. (ed.) (1996) *Training for Work in the Early Years*, Report of the Early Years Training Group. London: National Children's Bureau.

Selleck, D. and Goldschmied, E. (1996) Communication between babies – video resource pack. London: National Children's Bureau.

Siraj-Blatchford, I. (1996) Language, culture and difference: challenging inequality and promoting respect, in C. Nutbrown (ed.) *Respectful Educators – Capable Learners, Children's Rights and Early Education*. London: Paul Chapman.

Trevarthen, C. (1992) An infant's motives for speaking and thinking in the culture, in A. H. Wold (ed.) *The Dialogue Alternative*. Oxford: Oxford University Press.

UNICEF (1989) *Convention on the Rights of the Child*. New York: United Nations.

Vilien, K. (1993) Pre-school education in Denmark, in T. David (ed.) *Educational Provision for our Youngest Children: European Perspectives*. London: Paul Chapman.

Woodhead, M. (1996) In search of the rainbow, *Early Child Development Practice and Reflections*, 10. The Hague: Bernard Van Leer Foundation.

Introduction

Goldschmied and Jackson (1994: 1) claim that a society 'can be judged by its attitude to its youngest children, not only in what is said about them but how this attitude is expressed in what is offered to them as they grow up'. Each of the contributors to this book, whether they write as parent, university lecturer, nursery manager, researcher or teacher, has some powerful things to say about what is offered to the under-threes. They write about their own experiences and the ways in which their beliefs are translated into practice. Throughout there is a strong emphasis on the ways in which the needs of children should influence what they are offered; there is a continual recognition of the children's entitlement to respect, both as young learners and as people in their own right. Although the focus of both this book and *Working with the Under-threes: Training and Professional Development* is clearly on the adults involved, the voices of the children come through strongly.

Chapter 1 is written from the perspective of a working parent and explores one rationale for choosing childminding in preference to other forms of educare. The views and practice of one childminder are interwoven with a discussion of general issues, and there is a particular focus on the child's developing sense of self. Some of the inequalities perpetuated by childminding's position in the unsubsidized private end of the day care market are explored. The chapter by Fiona Fogarty explores similar issues and comes to very different conclusions.

Moss (1996) refers to the 'perverse distinctions' in the UK and some other parts of Europe between 'childcare for working parents' and 'daycare as a service for children and families in need'. Governmental divide-and-rule attitudes to families have been at the heart of these distinctions. Sometimes childcare has been seen as a private matter and sometimes as a potential votewinner. Most of the writers here have experience of (or provide) both sorts of care, but it is interesting to note that these distinctions do not exist in other parts of the world.

Brenda Griffin picks up this theme in Chapter 2 when she reports on her part in a current research project on Educare for the Under Threes – Identifying Need and Opportunity. She has a particular interest in the development of children's personal identities; she presents some of her findings in this area based on research with educarers in Denmark, Sweden and Finland as well as the UK. Some of the similarities and differences between the UK and Scandinavian attitudes are explored. She contrasts case studies from two of the British establishments (where children are encouraged to experiment and get involved) with the sad story of underconfident Alex. Throughout the chapter she explores some important issues concerned with the development of self-esteem and self-image.

The international dimension is also present in Chapters 3 and 4, where Caroline Barratt-Pugh takes us on a journey through both time and space from the beginnings of her educare career as a nursery nurse in the 1970s, through teaching in primary schools, to lecturing at the Manchester Metropolitan University, and, finally, to Australia and her current research at Edith Cowan University in Perth. Alongside this physical journey she outlines the ways in which her understandings about the ways in which children learn written and spoken language have deepened and changed. Chapters 3 and 4 focus on the ways in which young children, some of whom are bilingual, learn to speak and become literate. Caroline discusses how educarers provide opportunities for oracy and literacy behaviours, the ways they model the process of speaking, writing and reading, and how they can be sensitive to the children's needs and culture. She stresses the importance of involving families and the broader community in order to make appropriate provision for these very young children; she also emphasizes the importance of educarers being aware of their own beliefs about literacy and oracy if they are to make sensitive assessments of children's progress.

Like Caroline, Julia Gillen is very interested in how children acquire and refine their linguistic repertoire. In Chapter 5 she ponders the implications of her young daughter's repetitions of the Humpty Dumpty nursery rhyme. Here she discusses repetition and routine and the ways in which children's behaviour can be seen to challenge Chomsky's influential ideas about language acquisition. She refers to her research on young children's telephone talk and suggests some practical activities which harness the language learner's need for repetition and routine.

Goldschmied and Jackson (1994: 3) talk about the importance of good quality care being based not just on knowledge but also on 'an imaginative understanding of the experiences and feelings of young children, especially when they are separated from their parents'. In Chapter 6 Hilary Renowden demonstrates some of the ways in which this sort of understanding can relate to children's creativity. She stresses the importance of careful observation and sensitive involvement when assessing children's needs and abilities. Her nursery aims to maximize young children's creativity with the aim of developing their confidence both as social beings and as learners. She includes short case studies and examples of children's art which illustrate the ways in which children respond to the rich and stimulating environment of the nursery. Like Jean Coward in *Working with the Under-threes: Training and Professional Development*, Chapter 3, Hilary finds schema spotting a useful diagnostic tool as well as a way to check on children's needs.

Ruth Holland is also the owner of a private nursery and, like Hilary, has been influenced by ideas about the value of heuristic play; she writes about ways in which treasure baskets and opportunities to explore materials without pressure to produce an adult-orientated product can facilitate learning. In Chapter 7 she discusses how working practice in her nursery has changed as a result of staff taking time in observing the children carefully, and then responding to their differing needs appropriately.

In Chapter 8 Brenda Kyle writes from a head teacher's perspective about the ways in which her very special integrated nursery meets a diverse range of needs. She focuses on the 'opportunity group' where parents and children are all welcome 'as part of a large happy family'. She emphasizes the need for parents to see themselves as experts on their children and the importance of them valuing their children as people not children with labels. The provision for play is described as well as the ways in which the nursery communicates with and listens to parents and a wide range of other professionals. An underlying theme is the empowerment of parents and their children.

Chapter 9 is both similar and very different to Chapter 1. Both Fiona Fogarty and Helen Moylett write as parents having to choose day care for their young babies. They both found the decision difficult, both had years of teaching experience and plenty of information: yet made different choices. Here Fiona writes about the process of deciding to place her daughter in a nursery where she is very happy. However, this chapter highlights some more of the inequities involved in a system which does not treat childcare as a right for all working parents. Having opted for a nursery rather than a childminder, Fiona found there was only one accessible nursery which met the needs of working parents. The key issue with regard to equality of opportunity was that it happened to be private and therefore not available to many parents.

It is our view that all of the issues raised in this book warrant discussion at national level. In a very personal way each contributor demonstrates the importance – for all adults who work with young children – of being able to offer a considered response to key concerns in the early childhood field.

As Butler (1995: ix) says:

> Babies and children need, as they have always done, adults to love them, to care for them, laugh with them and help them learn. But many adults themselves find the world a bewildering place in which to function. Meeting children's needs, even if these can be identified, may seem impossibly difficult.

The adults writing or written about in this book would not claim to have found all the answers but they have all, in their different ways, reflected upon their practice in meeting children's needs and been courageous in facing issues and making changes. We hope that this collection of stories about children and adults and their early interactions will challenge readers and contribute to their future interactions with young children.

References

Butler, D. (1995) *Babies Need Books*, 3rd edn. London: Penguin.
Goldschmied, E. and Jackson, S. (1994) *People Under Three*. London: Routledge.
Moss, P. (1996) Defining objectives in early childhood services, *European Early Childhood Research Journal*, 4(1): 17–31.

1 | 'It's not nursery but it's not just being at home' – a parent and childminder working together

Helen Moylett

I returned to work when my son was 7 months old. On my first day back I left him playing happily with someone he had got to know gradually over the previous few weeks. From birth he had been used to relating to, and being left with, different adults and children. I did not expect him to be distressed when I left him. I made a good show of being happy and confident, and indeed parts of me were feeling happy and confident, but much more of me seemed to be feeling bereaved. That day, and on many others, I wept in the car on the way to work.

I suspect that this paragraph could have been written by almost any working mother. Wherever we live; however rich or poor; however supportive our partners, families and friends; whatever our beliefs about child-rearing; however strong our self-esteem – we all had to make a choice about work and then had to look for day care for our children. Then we had to cope with the practical and emotional consequences.

This chapter explores some of the issues associated with the choice of one particular form of day care – childminding. It draws on my own experiences as a parent and uses my relationship with one childminder to look at concerns which are relevant to many other parents and childminders. An important theme running through it, and discussed in more detail towards the end, is the development of the child's sense of self.

Firstly, some personal details will help contextualize the choices I was making. I had Connor, my first child, at the relatively advanced age of 38. Maternity leave was my first break from full-time work since I was 22. I have always enjoyed the job of teaching, whether in primary school or university and, for me, the personal and professional are very close: much of my self-esteem derives from success at work. Despite this I had very mixed feelings about returning to work. I was really enjoying full-time motherhood. I had met several new friends with young babies, and, in some ways, I envied those who were planning to stay at home full-time; in other ways they made me feel guilty about wanting to work. But want to work I did. Financially it would have been very difficult for me not to work, I also knew that I needed to have an identity outside the home and family, to be part of my profession. At the same time I knew I loved Connor very deeply and did not want to leave him. This ambivalent mix of feelings and needs informed my choices about Connor's day care.

Readers may have noticed that I mentioned earlier *my* choices and working 'mothers' rather than 'parents'. Although Connor's father is a very caring involved parent and we discussed all the options, we both saw the major responsibility as mine. Maternity leave also meant that I was the one with the time to think about decisions and visit people. This mirrors the general expectation in western industrialized societies that mothers take responsibility for their young children. As David (in David *et al.* 1993: 2) points out, 'This broad picture of primary maternal responsibility holds true regardless of women's marital status, employment position, ethnic group or social class.' Moss (1996: 252) refers to the way in which parental involvement in early childhood services usually means mothers' involvement, and regrets the general neglect of gender differences in discussion about parental involvement. He cites reports about services that do actively seek to encourage fathers' involvement but concludes that 'much more needs to be done to make early childhood services "father friendly" and to turn fathers into active stakeholders'. One can hardly disagree with him, although responsibility for such huge changes must be collective, requiring enormous cultural shifts. Phillips (1993: 9), for instance, points to the way in which female role models for girls have changed tremendously in the last 20 years, whereas for boys 'the situation has not changed in the same way. The men they see around them are not radically different to the men whom their fathers would have seen . . . they still do little housework and spend less time with their children than their wives do.' As Leach (1994: 13) wryly indicates, 'Most Western children get equal parenting the way Alice got jam in Alice in Wonderland: yesterday and tomorrow, but never today'!

I have briefly discussed these ideas about the construction of mothering roles because they underpin much of our collective understanding of childminding. Choosing a childminder means choosing another mother for one's child. This may seem an exaggerated view to those who see childminders more as paid educare workers than as mother figures, and I explore these ideas more thoroughly later in the chapter. However, it is interesting to note that there appears to be little chance of choosing a male childminder. The world of early years education is predominantly female, male educarers are rare (see Chapter 5 in *Working with the Under-threes: Training and Professional Development* for a male perspective on working with the under-threes); male childminders are like hen's teeth!

I recognize how lucky I was to have several educare options available. Although, like many other people these days, neither my partner nor I have parents or other relatives living nearby; we live in an area which is relatively well provided with day care and we could afford to pay for it. As Moss (1996: 19) emphasizes, 'most young children in the UK depend on an unsubsidised private market for the supply of services'. Surveys have revealed that most children under 3 with working parents are cared for by relatives, followed by childminders. The National Childminding Association figures show that over 300,000 under-fives spend part or all of every weekday with a registered childminder. There has been little recent research which has looked in any depth at the reasons for parents' choices and their attitudes and expectations about their children's day care. As Warner (1994) points out, it is difficult to ascertain why so many parents choose childminders in preference to other services such as nurseries or nannies – their reasons may be more pragmatic than ideological. My own reasons for choosing childminding, in preference to other forms of educare, were certainly ideological and will be explored presently.

As a prelude it might be useful to consider some research carried out by Long *et al.* (1996). This was a response to the general lack of reported studies which explore parents' attitudes and expectations about their choice of day care. The researchers analysed the responses of 275 parents – 273 mothers and two fathers (another indication that in the early years field, 'parent' usually means 'mother'!) – to an open-ended survey. Although one must be cautious about their conclusions based on such an opportunity sample (might reported parental ideas about the importance of educational – in preference to social activities for instance – have been influenced by parental perceptions of the researchers as educationalists?), one is left with some interesting questions about parental motivation.

The majority of parents were happy with their day care choice. Reasons for their choice were often pragmatic: affordability and flexibility of hours, for instance. The survey also attempted to investigate parents' knowledge of activities carried out during day care and where they obtained this knowledge.

The researchers expressed concern about the relative importance parents attached to the activities they were aware of. Social interaction was not seen as particularly valuable although we (the experts) know it is fundamental to cognitive and emotional development. There seemed to be little awareness that social values were an important part of childcare – in combating sexism and racism, for example. There was also little mention of the children's reactions to the care received. Parents were generally confident that they had enough information to make a choice about childcare, although the majority said they would have liked more beforehand. They had usually obtained information from friends rather than experts.

Although there were limitations to this study, it raises some interesting issues about the pressures on parents and the way in which they are seen by the 'experts'. It might be appropriate at this point to ponder what Penelope Leach says about the sort of expert colonization of parenting that is a consequence of the separation of parents' work from children's care:

. . . children have lost their taken-for-granted presence in, and apprenticeship to, what adults see as the most important aspect of their lives. Instead of spending much of childhood watching, 'helping' and emulating a range of adult people doing adult things, Western children spend it in special environments designed to keep them out of harm's and adults' way: children's worlds, staffed by people – usually women –

for whom childcare or education is paid work and therefore valued more highly than the personal care of parents.

(Leach 1994: 20)

Long *et al.*'s research would seem to indicate that parents do indeed have a tendency to undervalue ordinary social interaction as educational.

As I said earlier, my reasons for choosing a childminder for Connor were ideological; in fact, because I felt so strongly that childminding was what both he and I needed, I did not even visit available nurseries or consider nannies. That might seem an intolerant or unfair attitude to many readers, and possibly a little surprising coming from one of the editors of a book full of examples of good practice in a range of educare settings. It might also seem strange that somebody who might be seen as some sort of expert in early education should choose educare in a setting that requires no formal qualifications from practitioners and no special premises. However, although I recognize the vast amount of wonderful work that goes on in all sorts of educare establishments and the importance of our youngest children having access to committed and well-qualified staff, I did not want my son to attend an institution.

'Institution' might seem an unkind word to use about some of the informal educare establishments which feature elsewhere in this book, but I believe the best childcare is loving, responsive and individualized; the sort of care that is very hard to give in a routinized group setting – which even the best nurseries must necessarily be. My son was a baby who had so much learning to do; I believed that his learning could be best facilitated in a loving home environment. There is some research which has shown that children cared for in home settings tend to have more vocal communication directed at them and that this may lead to faster rates of language development (see for example Melhuish 1991). However, it seems likely that the quality of interaction between educarer and child is the crucial factor. I felt that this quality would be easier to assess in one individual childminder than in a nursery where there are several educarers. As Goldschmied and Jackson (1994: 74) say, 'Good care by one person is almost certain to be more loving and sensitive than care by a number of different people, however competent. The key person system is only a partial attempt to compensate for this inherent disadvantage of group care.'

Connor's immediate family consists of his parents and his two much older half-sisters and half-brother. I was therefore keen that he got used to relating to other very young children in a family setting. This effectively ruled out a nanny.

I have a great deal of sympathy with Leach's view of the separation of parents' work from children's care. I felt I wanted Connor to be engaged in 'real' life for as long as possible: to be with an adult doing her job, running her house, visiting her friends, going shopping, as well as engaging in specifically child-centred activities.

I started searching for a registered childminder who had young children of her own, who had loving and respectful attitudes to children and who would provide a stimulating environment matched to my child's needs. There is not space here to talk about the variety of childminders Connor and I met during that search, and the things that put me off or drew me to certain minders. However, it did help me to understand some of the reasons some parents might find it easier to place their child in a nursery!

Although social services registration means that the childminder's premises and resources have been inspected and found to be appropriate for up to three full-time children under 5, and that she has received some basic training, it has to be a baseline from which to start, rather than an assurance of excellence. Childminders rarely have glossy brochures and useful jargon-laden phrases for reassuring (or intimidating?) anxious parents; they rarely have strings of impressive-sounding qualifications or large super-hygienic houses with different areas for different activities. It is no easy task to go to somebody else's home and chat with them about their job and the way they see it; or to remember to ask the questions one feels one needs to ask and then, using the data gained, to make a decision about one's beloved child. I suppose I found it easier than some, because over the years I have gained a fair amount of experience in home visiting and interviewing. Nevertheless, the emotional investment I had in this decision making process made it very stressful.

In the end I found a good childminder, relationships seemed to be developing well and then, after a couple of months, she told us that she would be unexpectedly leaving Manchester. (Institutions, of course, do not tend to do this!) Luckily one of her friends had a vacancy for a full-time child. This friend already knew Connor and had expressed interest in minding him; she had also been previously recommended to me by two other mothers. Desperately worried about continuity of care, I went to see her and was reassured. She talked about my 9-month-old baby as a person she was fond of, and she and I liked each other immediately. So began a relationship with Mags and her family which has been, and continues to be, a source of support, education and care for both Connor and myself.

I am now going to explore some of the aspects of that relationship which seem to make it work for Connor, Mags and myself. Although this exploration is based on our particular childminding relationship the issues raised are relevant to many educare situations.

I claimed earlier that choosing a childminder was choosing another mother for one's child. On one level that can be taken as an unambiguous statement of fact – the overwhelming majority of childminders are mothers who have young children of their own.

However, I would like to explore some of the implications of wanting to have one's child 'mothered' by someone else.

Mothering is about loving and, for me, being a mother has certainly been a love story. However I have never believed in the soft focus, roses round the door, happy ever after sort of love stories (however powerful such fantasies may be!). Relationships may begin with hearts and flowers, but to survive they usually need compromise and commitment. Babies are neither sugar-coated bundles of joy; nor screeching sleep deprivers – two of the most common stereotypes on the birth congratulations cards! They are people with rights and feelings and the capability to do much and become more.

They, like all humans, need to be loved when they are in very sharp focus – behaving angrily for example, 'having an off day', or not being very obviously loving themselves. They also need to be loved when they are quietly sleeping, 'being a good girl' or saying their first words. In other words they need people who can offer unconditional love; who are consistently loyal; whose own self-esteem is well anchored. Through this loving behaviour they learn how to be loving themselves – to love both themselves and others. Years of being a teacher has led me to believe very strongly that children need loving role models who treat them as individuals worthy of respect, if they are to learn and grow up to become loving adults themselves.

All this may sound obvious to the point of banality, but we are all powerfully influenced by traditional constructions of childhood – some of which are antithetical to the position advanced above. Take the concept of original sin (with its attendant notion of the inherent wickedness of children) and the idea of children as adult property as examples. How many times have you heard a new mother being asked 'Is he good?' as if a new-born baby *could* be good or bad. What the questioner usually wants to know is how much inconvenience this new arrival is causing its owner. It may only be a year or so before this same child is hearing himself described as a naughty boy and is being regularly smacked by his parents; parents who would regard smacking another adult as completely out of order. How often have you heard two adults talking negatively about children over their heads as if they were not present? These smackers and chatterers have one thing in common – a disregard for the rights of the child. They would not smack another adult or talk about them in that way, either because they would not dare – an adult could hurt them back – or because they would think it abusive or socially inappropriate.

Earlier I wrote that I was looking for a childminder who had loving and respectful attitudes to children – who was definitely not a smacker or chatterer. I wanted this second mother to have ideas like mine about loving and learning, and to love my child in similar ways to myself. I wanted Connor to be getting consistent messages about his worth in the world. Some mothers I know told me that they did not really want this for their children; they worried about their children loving the childminder 'too much', resulting in less love for them. My belief is that we all have an infinite capacity for love and being loved, and the more loving we are exposed to the better. Goldschmied and Jackson (1994: 39) refer to some parents needing help 'to understand that sharing love and affection with another caregiver is not like sharing an apple or a sandwich where the more people the less there is for each'.

During the first conversation I had with Mags she was careful to tell me that she treated the children she minded as her own and 'loved' them, and that this meant kissing and cuddling. When I reacted positively to this statement she explained that some parents did not like this and she felt she had to make it clear that she could not mind children if she was 'not allowed to love them'. Mags has one daughter (Anna May), the same age as Connor, and another who is five years older. She and her husband are very openly affectionate with each other and their children, and the words 'I love you' are often heard. However, before any cynical reader begins to feel a trifle nauseated by all this sweetness and light, let me emphasize that Mags is no superhuman paragon of virtue who never gets cross or tired. One of the first sentences Connor uttered was 'Me a bit cross and I mean it!' which was more or less a direct quote from Mags. Mags and I both feel that part of loving is being real!

It must be apparent that one of the reasons that I felt happy to leave my child with Mags was because she had similar ideas about the practice of mothering to my own. However, what about the huge difference between us encapsulated by Mags when she said 'it must be so hard for you. I'm doing this job because I just can't leave my child'? As Ferri (1992: 68) indicates:

> The employed mother who places her child in the care of a childminder is doing something which the minder would never do herself. The child-minder, on the other hand, by remaining at home with her own children, is pursuing a course, which the mother, either from choice or necessity, has decided against. This distinction is of fundamental importance to the way in which minders and mothers perceive each other's role, and is likely to be a key factor in the way in which relationships develop.

Ferri's research involving the compilation of detailed case studies of 30 child-minding relationships led her to make that statement, which gets to the emotional core at the heart of the parent–childminder relationship.

Mags and I were lucky in that we liked each other as soon as we met. We share some important commitments to young children and their educare; we both refuse to take life too seriously and are tolerant of each other's occasional disorganizations. We are both extrovert, upfront types of people who like to get any concerns out in the open. I believe that these similarities must have made our relationship easier, while still not wishing to minimize the potential conflicts embedded within it.

Earlier in this chapter I mentioned the ways in which parenting of young children is still seen to be mothers' responsibility. Mags and I, like all mothers (and fathers) are influenced by current political and social constructions of mothers and working women. To summarize some of these crudely: on the one hand we hear statements about children's needs for their mothers that have their origins in the work of people like Bowlby (1953), who talked about the importance for emotional and social development of natural attachment; and on the other, we are exhorted to contribute to the economy and become 'have it all' superwomen. One could read implied criticism into Mags's remark about how hard I must find it to leave my child: I can somehow abandon my child and endure the pain of that separation whereas she (being a more loving mother) cannot. Alternatively one could see it as an empathic statement which lets me know that she understands what I must be feeling. Yet again one might be able to read some envy into what she says. All these readings are no more nor less 'true' than each other, but they do point to some of the possible ambiguities involved in the child-minder–parent relationship. Roles are not always clear-cut; people may feel conflicting emotions. Neither of the mothers (childminder or parent) may feel that she is always 'doing the best' for her child.

At the beginning of the chapter I mentioned the guilt I experienced about wanting to work and my feeling of bereavement on leaving my son. Mags has helped me to cope with these feelings in various ways. Apart from empathy and a generally non-judgemental attitude she sets things up so that there is always time made for transitions – first thing in the morning and in the evening. During this time we talk and she tells me about what she and the children are going to be doing during the day, or about what has happened. It is during these times that I have got to know Mags and her family better. Sharing activities with the children and a cup of tea or a glass of wine with the childminder is a good way to find out about what my son experiences every day.

When, after a few months, I was able to negotiate part-time work, Mags did not in any way imply that I should have done this sooner; she merely said she understood why I needed to do it and observed that she loved Connor so much that she would miss him. I had been worried by the loss of income that this change would mean for Mags. Would she be able to find another part-time child for those two days? Would she really prefer not to have Connor part-time and replace him with another full-time child? Mags was adamant that she loved all of us – not just Connor, but me and his dad as well – and did not want to lose us. This situation brought home to me just how complicated the relationships involved in childminding can become. We have an emotional relationship based on our love for one child and we are friends – we think highly of each other. Nevertheless, we employ Mags, in the sense that we pay her – although we do not determine to any great extent what she does, and she draws up the contract between us. Penelope Leach (1994: 95) describes the parent–childminder relationship as 'an equal partnership based on what really matters – the child's well-being and happiness'. I think I would describe it somewhat differently. If it is really soundly based on the child's well-being and happiness it has more chance of being an effective partnership, but it can never be truly equal because various inequalities and tensions are structured into it.

To illustrate this let us look again at the economic basis of the relationship. In our case, and in many others, the parents are professional people with qualifications which enable them to earn sufficient salaries to make paying a childminder a realistic prospect. A National Childminding Association briefing (1996a) points out that nearly three-quarters of women with high educational qualifications are at work when their children are under 5, and quotes an OPCS survey which showed that childminding was the first choice for households where the occupation of the main wage earner was 'professional, employer/manager or white collar'. The picture seems to be different as regards the childminders – a smaller percentage of them and their partners have professional qualifications and/or jobs. Ferri (1992: 64) noted that day care arrangements may thus bring together two families from different socio-economic groups. Also the childminder is being paid a derisory wage for being totally responsible for the parents' beloved children, even though that wage usually represents a substantial part of the parents' income. This illustrates the kind of inequality perpetuated where the political climate encourages the 'unsubsidized private market' approach to childcare to flourish.

Warner (1994: 30) sums up both the political and the practical nature of this situation when she says:

> Childminding has been seen mainly as 'women's work' and often equated with parenting, so it has traditionally been poorly paid. Childminders have sometimes felt exploited when parents are late paying or refuse to pay for holidays, or when their child does not attend because of sickness, or when Social Services are late sending money for a sponsored child.

Mags and other childminders have told me some stories about parents' non-payment that make my toes curl. Why is it that some apparently caring, solvent parents do not always see paying for their child's day care as a priority? It would be too easy to brand them as 'nasty' people who do not care about their childminder's financial well-being. It seems likely that their actions stem more from their difficulty in recognizing childminding as a job, than from any personality defect. The chapter in Ferri (1992) entitled 'The Business of Childminding' includes some interesting anecdotes which illustrate childminders' and parents' differing views about payment and contracts. My own view as a parent is that the contract we have with Mags is very useful. Her rates of pay are clearly set out and have been helpful when trying to remember what happens during holidays or sickness for example. A contract is also an encouragement to treat the childminder as another professional person. Mags feels very strongly that the work she does is both important and of good quality; parents should appreciate that and treat her, both personally and financially, with respect. Consequently, however, they need to rate her job as highly as their own. I feel that I certainly do that, but – given the beliefs I have and the job I do – I would be likely to.

Childminders generally are in a difficult position as regards status. On the one hand, they want recognition, but on the other there are no formal entry qualifications required and only basic training is needed for registration. The training and qualification arguments are rehearsed elsewhere in this book and in *Working with the Under-threes: Training and Professional Development*, but I would like to draw readers' attention to the appendix to this chapter. This contains some of the information for parents provided by Jo, a Manchester childminder. You may think she makes childminding sound like nursery, and you might be interested that she says:

> I did have the opportunity of registering my childcare practice as a private nursery but was told that all 'household' furniture had to be replaced with equipment as in the play room. I chose not to continue this route because I felt it was very important for very young children to be in a home environment.

> (Mathieson 1996)

Looking back to my early interviews with childminders, this sort of documentation would certainly have made my life easier. It paints a picture of Jo's priorities, values and beliefs, and gives a strong impression that this is a childminder who takes her job very seriously. It also has the potential to educate parents who may be unaware of the importance of providing a range of experiences for their young children. (This seems to be what Long *et al.*'s research, mentioned earlier in this chapter, indicated.) However, my feeling is that there are dangers involved in advocating a status for childminding based on similarity to nursery. There has long been a tendency to look to the next stage in a child's life for a rationale and validation for current practice. One has to look no further than the effect of the National Curriculum on nursery practice.

Most recent writings about quality in early childhood provision have referred to the way values and beliefs influence relationships and interactions – and, therefore, the quality of the educare – more significantly than any other factor (see, for example Abbott and Rodger 1994; Moss and Pence 1994; Moss 1996). Moss (1996) talks about the importance of valuing diversity within an inclusive model of childcare services. He points to the dangers inherent in regarding these services as either businesses or vehicles for delivering national programmes.

Of course no amount of brochures with appropriate-sounding phrases will actually ensure quality of provision. So how do I judge the quality of the educare Connor is receiving when he is with Mags? How do I know that the values she talked about when I first met her are translated into some sort of daily reality for my son? On a simple level I know that he is loved. I can see that in the way he and Mags interact and the ways in which he talks about her. Although he is always pleased to see me or his father, he is often reluctant to leave Mags's house, particularly if he is involved in something interesting. 'I love Magsy', he often says. She and the rest of her family are always included in his lists of people he loves. (He is now 2 and very keen on listing things.) Recently, when helping me get ready to go to Sainsbury's, he wrote a shopping list which included presents for Mags and her daughter.

On another simple level I know he is playing with all sorts of appropriate and stimulating resources and toys, both at Mags's house and at the various toddler groups she both organizes and attends. I know resources are chosen with equal opportunities in mind – there are no 'boys" and 'girls" toys and there are positive images of people from a variety of cultures. I know they read lots of stories and go to the library for story sessions. But what about the more complex values underlying interaction with people and resources, the hidden curriculum? Presumably at this stage it is less hidden than it will be when we come into contact with the institutions that he will eventually attend. It's hard to hide your real values from someone who enters your home several times a week in an informal way.

I want Connor to be confident in himself and to grow up respecting other people. The first step to respect for others is respect for oneself, and Mags works hard to allow the children she cares for to develop their sense of individuality and autonomy. This can be seen in all sorts of small ways. She believes in the value of exploratory play and allows the children to explore materials in their own way – they can set the agenda, everything is not structured by her. Connor feels quite comfortable experimenting with face painting and telling everyone, 'When I a bit older I going to have perfume, lipstick and mascara for my own'; nobody has implied that this is an inappropriate choice for a boy. Of course one could say that Connor is inhabiting an unusually female world at Mags's (and probably an unusually liberal one at home) and that sooner or later he is going to be confronted with the reality of the ways in which mainstream maleness is constructed in the world. Phillips (1993) has some powerful things to say about the ways in which boys become men and the implications for their parents. In a chapter entitled 'Mother Power' she warns of the potential problems looming for mothers and sons when the son encounters 'other children and adults, who may have a more developed sense of gender and need to enforce those divisions to prop up their own identity'. All I can hope is that when Connor does begin to realize that others have expectations of him based on his sex, that his early years will have built some solid rock beneath the shifting sand of experience.

Mags gives the children choices as often as possible about small things, like which biscuit they want; which car seat they will sit in; which story they would like; which colour felt pen to use. When their wants conflict, ways of sharing fairly are discussed and the rationale explained. Mags answers all questions as honestly and fairly as she can and she is tolerant of the children's feelings – they are allowed to be angry or upset, for instance. She has few rules, but she applies them consistently and, when conflict occurs, uses various strategies such as distraction, negotiation, firmness and occasionally, shouting. Connor does a good imitation of her warning the children that this might happen: 'Now do I have to shout?' He tells me he does not like it when this happens. He still occasionally recalls an incident when he, Anna May and another child pulled a lot of flower heads off. 'Mags did shout and we cried 'cos we was very naughty and them lovely flowers they was all gone aahh!' He often says to me 'Don't look at me like that, I don't like it!', but he is quick to say 'Sorry' and amend his behaviour. My belief is that this is partly because he has not been treated aggressively either at Mags's or at home; adults being cross or shouting means that he has overstepped a serious boundary. I hope he will grow up to be appropriately assertive – the way in which he is asked to make decisions already and the way in which his choices are respected should help that process.

Already he believes that he can influence adult behaviour in quite subtle ways, not just by crying or shouting. He has learned to say 'excuse me' when he interrupts conversation. When this is repeated very forcefully and with rising volume if ignored, it is usually a successful opening gambit. On one recent occasion he had been told that his dad and I were having a serious conversation which he must not interrupt. His response to this was to go away and make some marks on a piece of A4 paper which he then brought into the room and held up. When we inevitably stopped talking to look at it, he announced 'This says please be quiet.' He also uses 'adult' behaviour to regulate adult actions. The other day, for example, I asked him if he wanted me to read his Fireman Sam comic with him and he said 'This is not a comic, this is my newspaper and I am reading about that train on fire [a reference to an article in that day's *Guardian*], you be quiet now.' Another time he was making marks on paper and I asked him what he was doing and he said 'This is very important. I am going to school with this picture, I am Emily [Mags's elder daughter].' He also often says he is 'doing work' when he is writing or reading. Mags is a qualified hairdresser, and he makes her sit still while he 'does' her hair. These are more than amusing anecdotes; they show that Connor is a child who believes he has some control over his world and some access to that adult world of work that Leach regrets is so often denied to children these days.

Obviously at the age of 2 he is fairly egocentric but he knows and meets a range of adults and young people via his family; Mags has friends from all sorts of backgrounds and is always very positive about the diversity of society and different ways of life. I know from the way in which she speaks, the friends she has, the resources she provides, that she recognizes the harm that discrimination based on prejudice does. Mags also minds children for social services and sometimes undertakes emergency short-term caring. This has meant Connor meeting people who are much more distressed than others he is used to, but Mags has always talked about all the children's behaviour in a positive way and he appears to take everything in his stride. The messages he is getting are all about valuing himself and others; he is beginning to develop empathy. Recently Mags's elder daughter was off school and Connor told me that she 'had a poorly tummy and she was in bed and me and Anna May we did give her cuddles to feel her better . . . I been sick once . . . it was horrid'. The other day he came and stood in the doorway of the room where I was working. A tape of Chopin nocturnes was playing in the background. The next minute he was leaning his head against me asking, 'Oh mummy, are you sad?' I responded by saying 'No, why do you ask that?' to which he replied, in a very sad small voice, 'This music very sad, I don't like it, turn it off.'

So far I have painted a very positive picture of this educare relationship – but what about the inevitable differences between home and childminders? As a parent, I came to the conclusion long ago that we can all live quite happily with all sorts of differences between what happens at home and at the childminder's as long as they are not differences in values and beliefs. My view is that small differences remain small if one keeps that perspective.

Of course any child being part of two different households will notice differences. For instance, very soon after he could walk and climb he was told that he was not allowed to climb on the kitchen table at home. However, at Mags's he and Anna May were allowed to climb up and walk around on the table. He went through a period of climbing onto Mags's table as soon as I arrived to collect him and standing smiling at me. Mags and I dealt with this by just acknowledging what he was doing and saying that we knew that he was not allowed to do this at home. I assume that seeing us discussing it calmly and the fact that he was receiving a consistent (if different) message from both of us, helped him come to terms with this and other differences between home and his childminder's.

He certainly understands that there are appropriate behaviours linked to different places. When we were returning from the library recently he said 'I was a bit noisy in there and running around – you didn't mind [remind] me first and I forgotten.' When I asked what I didn't remind him about he replied, 'About being quiet.' When talking about a trip to work with his father he said, 'I played with my toys and done some work on daddy's pooter [computer] and I be very quiet when daddy talking with those people . . . you not allowed to do shouting at work.'

Of course as a proud parent I am biased, but it seems to me that Connor is developing respectful and loving attitudes and an appreciation of others' feelings. He also feels that he is important and that his opinions matter. I am sure that because he has been so well loved, educated and cared for by his childminder, it has contributed enormously to this development. Mags sees childminding as a balancing act: 'It's not nursery but it's not just being at home – you've got to think about what the children need as well, that's my job.' Ferri (1992: 160) points to the importance of this balance when thinking about childminder training and talks about the need 'to address the underlying issue of how far the childminder's role should be, in the broadest sense, explicitly educative, or – as so widely seen by its practitioners – one of recreating the ethos of the home environment'.

It seems to me that Mags manages to achieve an appropriate balance, not just because she is aware of the importance of providing learning experiences, but because she sees everyday life in the home environment as a learning experience. I recently watched her making rhubarb crumble with Connor, Anna May and another toddler. All three were standing on chairs at the work surface in the kitchen with Mags in the middle using a sharp knife to chop the rhubarb. While the children watched her chop, while they were exploring the pieces of rhubarb and then, when they were all engaged in transferring the rhubarb to the pan, Mags encouraged them to talk about how the rhubarb grew, where it had come from, grandad's allotment, why they had to remove the leaves, why they cannot yet use sharp knives, what was going to happpen to the rhubarb in the pan, how they could tell how much sugar to use, when they would make the crumble mixture and lots more relevant issues. Connor and Anna May joined in enthusiastically, contributing their ideas and listening to the others. Connor felt confident to contribute details about the rhubarb in our garden and what he could remember about crumble making. Mags was careful to create space for the other younger, less confident child to speak and also checked that she understood what had been said. This short anecdote seems to me to illustrate an approach to childminding which sees the educational potential in everyday life; which is responsive to individual children's needs and which depends both on a belief in children's ability to get involved in adult life, and on a respect for the contribution they make to it.

Mags and I both feel that our shared views of the world in general, and the development of young children in particular, have helped us to build and maintain a relationship based on mutual trust and understanding. Although our jobs are different, we respect each other on a personal and professional level and have avoided some of the potential areas of conflict explored earlier. In various ways we have supported each other in a relationship which is loving and friendly but also formal and contractual. At the moment the plan is that this will probably come to an end when both our children are 3 1/2 and we will, somewhat reluctantly, send them to nursery. For both of us and our children this will mark the end of an era in our lives and the beginning of whole new sets of relationships. I hope they will be as happy.

References

Abbott, L. and Rodger, R. (eds) (1994) *Quality Education in the Early Years*. Buckingham: Open University Press.

Bowlby, J. (1953) *Child Care and the Growth of Love*. Harmondsworth: Penguin.

David, M., Edwards, R., Hughes, M. and Ribbens, J. (1993) *Mothers and Education: Inside Out?* Basingstoke: Macmillan.

Ferri, E. (1992) *What Makes Childminding Work?* London: National Children's Bureau.

Goldschmied, E. and Jackson, S. (1994) *People Under Three*. London: Routledge.

Leach, P. (1994) *Children First*. London: Penguin.

Long, P., Wilson, P., Kutnick, P. and Telford, L. (1996) Choice and childcare: a survey of parental perceptions and views, *Early Child Development and Care*, 119: 51–63.

Mathieson, J. (1996) Assignment contributing to assessment for BA (Honours) Early Childhood Studies. Manchester Metropolitan University.

Melhuish, E. C. (1991) Research on day care for young children in the United Kingdom, in E. C. Melhuish and P. Moss (eds) *Day Care for Young Children: International Perspectives*. London: Routledge.

Moss, P. (1996) Defining objectives in early childhood services, *European Early Childhood Research Journal*, 4(1): 17–31.

Moss, P. and Pence, A. (1994) *Valuing Quality in Early Childhood Services*. London: Paul Chapman Publishing.

National Childminding Association (1996a) *Briefing re. Daycare Services in England*. London: NCMA.

National Childminding Association (1996b) *Briefing on Nursery Education and Grant Maintained Schools Bill*. London: NCMA.

Phillips, A. (1993) *The Trouble with Boys, Parenting the Men of the Future*. London: Pandora.

School Curriculum and Assessment Authority (1996) *Desirable Outcomes for Children's Learning*. London: DfEE and SCAA.

Warner, J. (1994) Childminders and children, in T. David (ed.) *Working Together for Young Children*. London: Routledge.

Appendix

Jo Mathieson
NNEB
Registered childminder

Dear parents

What will your child be doing,
while in my care? What will they learn? What will be provided for them? Will
your child's individual needs be met? What experience and knowledge does
your childminder have?

These are very common questions, asked by the majority of parents: those
who come to me for a placement, those who come to me for information and
advice (I run a vacancy scheme in the area), and sometimes those who are
unsure about their child's childminder.

I have, therefore, written these notes for your information – regarding my
child care practice. They will explain my approach to child care, health and
development. They give you information about each area/activity your child
will be involved in and the developmental values and benefits.

Hopefully, this will generate more questions and ideas from yourself – read
it, think about it and let me know your views.

My experience and knowledge
I am a qualified Nursery Nurse and have been working with young children
for over 14 years. During this time, I have learnt and come to understand a
great deal about children: the various stages of development, how they
behave, how they acquire knowledge and skills, how they build an understanding of the world around them – the basic ingredients needed to meet
the challenges that face them as they grow.

I am aware of what is required, by me the educator, to assist their development at each stage in their early years.

I have seen and experienced the many difficulties, problems, concerns and
worries that arise in the first years of life – for parents and children – and work
closely with parents to help overcome these challenges in a positive way.

Qualifications   NNEB in nursery nursing
                 Valid first aid till 1999
                 Special educational needs training
                 Various short course – related to early years

                 Currently undertaking a BA in early childhood studies

                 Are you reassured?

Why am I a childminder?
When I was expecting my daughter, I visited many childminders but could
not find one that provided the kinds of things I wanted for my daughter.
I was, as you would imagine, quite concerned, amazed, worried . . . I didn't

feel that my expectations were any different to any other parent's. I had my son, 13 months later, and had already decided to leave my job (in a nursery) and become a childminder myself – providing what I felt was the right environment and setting for young children of working parents.

My aim

Each child is an individual and will grow and develop at their own pace. My aim is to provide them with all the experiences and opportunities I can, in order for them to grow to their full potential. I feel it is important for young children to be in an environment where they can interact well with the adults and children, build their communication skills with confidence, express their individuality confidently and build a good attachment with their childminder. Children learn through play. What is 'play' and what is 'learning'?

PLAY is the method by which children gain all the knowledge, skills and understanding they need to fulfil their potential. Play is fun, exciting, productive.

LEARNING is the process of absorbing information, experiences, opportunities and concepts to develop emotionally, physically, intellectually, linguistically, socially and creatively.

My aim is to assist this by providing a variety of activities and experiences to allow each child to: have fun, learn new skills, experiment, use their senses to understand and gain knowledge, explore a variety of concepts and ideas and collect information about their world and the people around them, in a safe, warm and stimulating home environment.

WHAT I DO
YOU ARE YOUR CHILD'S FIRST EDUCATOR – I AM THEIR SECOND

I believe in working in partnership with parents to provide the best for each child in my care.

I operate a 'open door' policy – parents are always welcome to join in with activities and stay for as long as they wish. I respect the parents I work with – after all, you know your child better than anyone else. Your views, ideas, comments, etc. are valuable and I feel that it is very important for me to be able to work with you in partnership.

I am always available and like to spend as much time as possible with parents. It is very important for your child to be able to see that Mum/Dad and childminder can communicate well, make time to talk, respect each other and can work as a team to provide continuity of care. This builds your child's confidence, sense of security and promotes a happy child. Having gone through this situation myself, I am fully aware of the worries, anxieties and concerns parents feel when leaving their child with a childminder.

I encourage equal opportunities – each child should have the opportunity to develop to his or her full potential regardless of race, origin, sex, disability, cultural or social background. Each child is an individual, and his or her needs, wishes and ideas should be met. We live in a multi-cultural, multi-racial society and the children of today will be the adults of tomorrow – promoting equality of opportunity and opposing discrimination of any kind will help them to combat these injustices in later life. Children pick up ideas and values from the adults around them. My aim is to promote positive views and ideas. Amongst my equipment you will see: positive images, through books, posters, activities. Artefacts in the home corner. Black and male dolls. Asian and other dressing-up items.

I use language that does not discriminate or influence stereotypes.

Discipline

I do not smack or use any form of physical punishment. Instead, I use the 'time out' method to encourage positive behaviour. What is time out? Removing the child from the conflicting situation, diverting their attention, reassuring and comforting them, teaching right from wrong in a positive way. I feel it is important for myself and the parents to work together to encourage positive behaviour, so the child does not face conflicting ideas and values.

Outings

I take the children to three drop-in sessions each week – I am key holder and organizer for these sessions. Attending the drop-in enables the children to build their social skills and develop new relationships with other children who are also minded. It gives them an opportunity to use different equipment and materials, experience other surroundings and become familiar with facilities in the local environment. The children, all ages, enjoy these sessions very much.

I take the children on local 'discovery trips' – perhaps to reinforce a theme or activity we are doing or sometimes to follow a child's individual request or idea. This extends the child's learning process, familiarizes them with the local environment and gives them first-hand experience.

Routine

I feel it is important for children to have a routine – this helps children understand the concept of time. They become familiar with the events of each day. A good routine provides a sense of security, comfort and stability. When working with young children, flexibility is a must. Although the basic needs are always there – sleep time, meal time, snack times, free play time, structured activities – the children exercise freedom of choice about the activities they do, thus encouraging independence.

Individual needs

Children's needs vary according to a variety of factors, situations and circumstances. I make sure that each child in my care has my attention and understanding when needed, for as long as it is needed. The children build a strong relationship with me in a warm, comfortable, safe and stimulating environment. They also build a strong relationship with my assistant. Between us we can give each child all the love, warmth and attention they need, in a home environment with plenty of stimulating and enjoyable activities.

Under one

Babies require a lot of one-to-one attention. This is no problem as there are always two adults present. I feel it is also important for them to be part of the group and be involved in what is going on – not to be left in a chair, at a distance or separated from the other children. The baby is often with me, experiencing, watching and listening. Babies learn very quickly and, given the right kind of care and attention, they will thrive and develop quickly.

They build relationships with the other children and the older children learn to be considerate, caring, loving and become aware of the babies' needs. This is a valuable experience for both.

 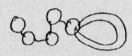 

My voluntary roles

I am an active member of the Manchester City Childminding Association, taking the role of voluntary Fund-raising and Social Officer. Within this role, I organize local fund-raising events, assist other childminding groups around Manchester to hold events and write short articles for the MCCMA news letter.

I am also a voluntary Link Visiting Officer for my area – I provide support and help to new childminders in my area, give them ideas and advice, encourage them to attend the drop-in sessions, reinforce issues discussed on the registration course – child safety, importance of play, equal opportunities, Manchester's no smacking policy – how to provide the best for the children in their care.

The children in my care come first and these voluntary roles do not take up my working time with the children.

For your information:

ACTIVITIES AND THEIR VALUES

Physical play – the garden is large and outdoor equipment is plentiful. I take children to the local park and outdoor play is also available during a drop-in session.

Values – enjoyment, release of surplus energy, offers new freedom from possible tension. Stimulates an appetite, digestion, circulation, sleep, mental alertness, skin health. Promotes muscle tone, coordination, manipulative skills, balance, control, body awareness, resistance to infection. Develops skills such as: running, stopping, climbing, jumping, etc. Offers elements of

challenge and adventure. Builds concepts of
height, width, spatial awareness, distance, speed.
Develops social skills, sharing, collaborating,
working together. Builds self-confidence. Stimulates intellectual curiosity, observation, aesthetic
awareness and a sense of wonder about animals
and nature. Encourages imaginative play.

Given a variety of equipment all these skills
will be met.

Sand and water play – these activities are provided every day when the
weather is fine. They are also provided at each drop-in session.
Values – enjoyment, sensory experience, release of tension, outlet for aggression and frustration, therapeutic values, language opportunities. Encourages
manipulative skills, builds imaginative development. Mathematical and scientific discoveries concerning: volume, capacity, floating, sinking, material
properties. Links with home life: holidays, other family events.

Clay and playdough – playdough is used almost every day, as asked for by the
children. Clay is used once or twice a fortnight.
Values – lots of enjoyment, endless possibilities – there is no right or wrong
way to use these materials. Emotionally an outlet for aggression, tension,
therapeutic values. Links with their own home environment – cooking. Scientific discoveries, properties of each material, effects when wet, dry. Satis-
fies curiosity, promotes questions, ideas. Opportunity for imaginative play.
Language development.

A variety of objects are introduced at each play session – to promote new
ideas and uses.

Imaginative play – a wide variety of materials and situation are set up to
encourage imaginative play – house corner, shop, hospital, cafe, post office,
etc. Each is well stocked with accessories. There is an outdoor play house with
kitchen area, bedroom, living room. Other materials and equipment are provided – dressing-up items, 'the real macoy' – and as a group we make large
play items such as cars, boats, buses, etc. Children develop their imaginative
skills in all the other areas/activities provided.
Values – enjoyment, develops social skills, helps child to understand people
and relationships. Encourages role play – what they see the adults around
them doing. Encourages manipulative skills, coordination, thinking skills,
problem solving. Provides an opportunity to release frustrations, anger,
other emotions. Helps children to come to terms with areas of concern, fear,
difficulty. Provides an insight into adult behaviour. Mathematical experiences, sensory experiences, stimulates language development. Helps children learn about themselves – their abilities, their feelings, their likes and
dislikes – and lots, lots more!

Cooking activities – I bake with the children at least once a week. We make a variety of things for tea times, snack times and tea parties. If we make biscuits, small cakes, etc. the children take one home.

Values – enjoyment, linked with home, sensory experiences – feel, smell, taste. Provides an emotional release – beating, whisking, kneading. Mathematical experiences – shape, size, weight, capacity, counting, changes in texture, shape, effects of heat, cold. Provides an opportunity for language development. Early reading skills – labels, recipe books, etc. Social skills are developed. Understanding of food, nutritional information, hygiene, home safety, diet. Encourages concentration, thinking skills, observation skills. Produces an end product and encourages self-praise, self-ability.

Wonderful to watch them learn and absorb information through a cooking activity.

Creative activities – I keep a good stock of paints, glue, collage materials, a variety of papers and card. I collect items such as wool, fabric pieces, shells, cones, string, empty containers, feathers, bottle tops, lolly sticks, newspaper, computer paper, pastas, rice, beans, etc., old cards, paper plates, ribbon – in fact, anything I can use for creative activities.

Values – self-expression, freedom to discover, experiment, explore the properties of each medium. Enjoyment, release of tension, aggression. Opportunities to experience a variety of materials – some out of context. Encourages imagination, stimulates language development. Develops creative expression. Promotes self-awareness, self-appraisal, achievement. End product to show parents. Fosters tastes and personal preferences. No right or wrong way to use the materials. Perception of shape, texture, spatial relationships. Scientific learning – consistencies, colour mixing, effects of other materials. Stimulates language development. Avenue of expression. Sensory experiences. Promotes decision making, choice, independence, self-appraisal. It also introduces them to equipment such as brushes, glue spreaders, scissors, etc.

Creativity arises in many areas, not just by using paints, glue, etc.

Construction toys – Mobilo, Duplo, Lego, bricks, magnetic bricks, stickle bricks, linking cubes, Superstrato, etc.

Values – enjoyment, feeds imagination, language development, encourages social development. Gives first-hand experience in spatial relationships – next to, on top of, underneath. Introduction to three dimensions. Self-expression, self-awareness. Pleasure at own creations.

Construction occurs in many areas, not just with specific equipment.

Jigsaws, sorting, matching toys – lots of different items used.

Values – improves hand and eye coordination, fine manipulative skills, language development, social development, thinking skills, intellectual development and lots more!

Games – structured games outdoors, board games, lotto, matching games, recognition games, number games, etc. all stimulate intellectual development, social skills, thinking skills, imagination, language development, patience, consideration to others, listening skills, mathematical awareness, etc.

Children learn from everything they are involved with. If the adult is dedicated, enthusiastic, interested and gives children the attention, time and respect they require, the child will develop skills and understanding in each of the important areas.

Other activities – planting seeds, nature hunts, washing dolls and equipment, exploring nature, drawing, writing skills – using a variety of mediums – chalk, crayons, pastels, felt pens, charcoal sticks, fabric pens, to name just a handful!

Remember – babies come into the world with none of these skills – everything comes from experience and opportunities.

You may feel that your baby is too young for most of these activities – may I just add that babies from 5–6 months can engage in a number of these activities and develop their senses, early knowledge and understanding. Babies are not babies for long – so it is important for you to know what lies ahead for them.

Settling-in procedure
I feel it is very important for parent and child to spend as much time as possible with me before a childminding arrangement begins. I advise a staggered settling-in procedure, over a minimum of two weeks.

Book list for your information

The Growth and Development of Children – Catherine Lee, published by
  Longman
Child Care and Health – J. Brain and M. Martin, published by Hulton Educa-
  tional Publications
Child Development – A First Course – K. Sylva and I. Lunt, published by Basil
  Blackwell
Day Care – Alison Clarke-Stewart, published by Fontana Paperbacks
Discipline Without Shouting or Spanking – J. Wyckoff and B. Unell, published
  by Meadowbrook Books
People Under 3 – Young Children in Day Care – E. Goldschmied and S. Jackson,
  published by Routledge
The First Years of Life – Open University, published by Ward Lock
The Pre-school Child – Open University, published by Ward Lock

There are plenty of books on the subject of child care, under fives, child
development, play, etc.
   The above are part of my personal collection and are available should you
wish to borrow them.

Matheson.

Jo
  xx

Week beginning 14 July 1996

SPECIAL ACTIVITIES THIS WEEK

Don't throw out your newspaper – we are making a big train from large cardboard boxes and papier maché this week.
Jack's new word: 'train'
William went on a train for the first time over the weekend!
Got any train tickets?

Remember Phoebe? Sue and Phoebe are visiting Manchester on Wednesday and will be calling in during the afternoon – with baby Alex!

Friday – Andrew's birthday
4 years old. Tea party at tea time!

coloured in by
Laura

Sample weekly menu 5 May 1997

	Monday	Tuesday	Wednesday	Thursday	Friday
snack	Strawberry milkshake with apple and banana pieces	Toast fingers with peanut butter Milk – baby	Milk – baby Apple juice with marmite toast	Pure orange juice with homemade biscuits	Apple juice with biscuits
lunch	Fish cakes Carrots Mash Sponge cake and custard	3-bean hot pot Yoghurt	(veg.) Macaroni cheese (meat) Mince pie with peas and carrots Mash Yoghurt	Vegetable pastries Potato whirls Sauce Jelly and fruit	(veg.) Vegetable pie (meat) Chicken pie Mixed veg. Ice cream
tea	Cheese pasty Meat pasty	Sandwiches: – Veg. paste – Cheese paste Juice Fruit	Toasties Juice Lolly or ice cream	Pizza pieces Fruit juice Apple	Nibbles: – carrot sticks – cheese sticks Crackers Juice
notes	Veg. burger for Michael instead of Fish cake		No peas – Michael		

2 | 'The child should feel good enough' – nurturing a sense of self in young children

Brenda Griffin

Every child is a unique personality, I'd like to keep it that way.
(Pre-school teacher, Sweden)

When I met Alex for the first time in the late 1980s he was 17 months old. His mother held him tightly as she sat in my office discussing the nursery place Alex was about to take up at the centre and what Sue, his mother, expected from us, as his educarers.

Alex did not look at me throughout the 30 or so minutes we were together, nor did he make a sound. In fact, Alex's eyes stayed on his mother throughout and my attempts to encourage him to look, talk or play with me were clearly causing him to feel uncomfortable, and so I did not pursue this.

Several weeks later when Alex had settled into the centre and had begun to form a relationship with Ann, his key worker, we were noticing other behaviours that gave us cause for concern. Alex would not make eye contact with anyone other than Ann; he became very distressed when Ann was not available, he showed no interest in other children or what they were doing and his own attempts at play were very short-lived and created a frustration in him that required the calming that seemingly only Ann could offer.

Alex had many problems to contend with in his life and his story was not a happy one. What was very evident to us, the staff team who worked so hard to undo the harm he had experienced, was that at 17 months old, Alex had already reached some decisions about his own worth and abilities. His progress continued to be hampered by his lack of courage to try, and by the continued negative feedback he received (not from centre staff) on any attempts he made to express himself. Alex had learned to be quiet and still. He had learned that it was better not to try, he had learned he was 'not good enough'.

I use the story of Alex as a sad example of the misuse of power by adults towards children and as an introduction to a chapter that will explore the influential role of professional carers and educators (educarers) in young children's developing sense of themselves.

How do we, in a professional context, nurture the uniqueness that is the right of every individual? How do we professionally contribute to children's growing awareness of themselves as separate entities and their separate identities? How can we ensure that every child feels valued and 'good enough' to just be, and that they confidently attempt anything and enjoy the endeavour?

In attempting to respond to these questions, I will describe the practice of professional educarers, both in local settings and in selected mainland European countries where I have been involved in a recent research programme (Abbott and Gillen 1997).

The research project was designed to identify factors contributing to quality experiences for children under 3 in a range of group settings outside their own home. The investigation was planned to be completed in two years (1995–7) and aimed to collect information from the vast range of services offered to young children in Denmark, Sweden, Finland and the United Kingdom.

Through the use of a detailed questionnaire developed by the research team and, where possible, a structured interview schedule, we were able to solicit the aims, philosophies, purposes and practices of a wide variety of educare workers. In addition, locally in the North-West of England we were able to make focused observations of daily practices in a number of different early years settings.

While the aim was to gather information on a range of issues relating to the educare of children under 3, there were four main areas on which we concentrated. These were:

- ways in which children are helped to develop a personal identity;
- what constitutes a curriculum for under-threes;
- ways in which children's learning and development are assessed and the extent to which this influences provision;
- ways in which workers establish and maintain relationships with children and their parents.

My particular area of interest is the development of children's personal identities, but I have outlined the other areas which the team are researching because they are interrelated; I will be referring to them later in this chapter.

It is, of course, essential to recognize that all experiences are context related and that we should examine early childhood provision within the context of a society and its values. However, as members of the broader European early childhood community, we are all involved with the same questions and the search for answers.

One of the early and significant differences between the UK and Scandinavia was the response to the questions: 'What are your particular aims with regard to children under 3 years?' and 'Why are these important to you?'

There were major transnational variations in the aims which appeared to give some indication of the professional discipline and/or the type of training experienced by the respondents.

The following list of responses extracted from the UK questionnaire gives some indication of these variations:

- We provide curriculum areas.
- Staff plan for children's individual needs by recording and organizing play plans.
- We offer a broad curriculum. What each child gains from it is different because of age and ability.
- The younger children mix with older children. They need a high level of input from staff.
- We offer a higher ratio of staff to children, enabling a closer relationship.
- We provide play plans and room plans as a structure set by the staff teams for the day.
- We offer pre-reading and pre-writing skills within a smaller group setting as a preparation.
- To provide a stimulating and safe environment as well as ensuring happiness and adequate development for every child in our care.
- We provide an environment which reflects the home, domestic situation.
- The emphasis of care for under-threes is aimed at the social and emotional development of the child.

Playgroups discussed issues of security in terms of children being safe from harm; they talked of the importance of a routine and how this 'progressed' children to a more structured environment (school); they emphasized the development of children to reach their 'full potential': this was described as 'intellectual, sensory, social and emotional'. Physical care was also an important consideration.

Childminders again discussed the importance of a routine and were specific about hygiene, diet and rest issues; they talked about 'learning right from wrong', being prepared for the next stage (nursery or school), and having 'toys that are fun and educational'. Childminders felt they made a contribution to children's physical, intellectual, linguistic, emotional and social development by providing a 'happy, secure, safe, caring, comfortable, loving, stimulating and welcoming environment'.

Day nurseries/nursery centres responded in quite similar ways to the above but added to their answers the significance of a key worker system to enable trusting relationships to be formed, and the need to reflect the cultural diversity of the UK. Some centres discussed very specific curricula, designed to give 'choice and first-hand experiences'.

When considering the Scandinavian responses to the questionnaire it is important to remember that colleagues in Sweden, Denmark and Finland are not under any pressure to adopt a national early years curriculum. In Sweden, for instance, childcare programmes offer learning experiences under the headings: nature, culture and society. These are 'intended to support children's growing sense of identity, comprehension of the environment, and ability to communicate with others' (Bergman 1993: 123).

In Denmark, government both at national and local authority level does not require curriculum content from childcare centres, so this is left entirely in the hands of centre staff. The Child Welfare Commission (established 1974) formulated long-term goals for a policy on the child (1981). These were:

- to provide a happy secure environment where they will develop to their maximum potential;
- providing opportunities, experiences and materials to develop their physical, emotional, intellectual and language skills as fully as possible;
- to respect the child as an individual in the family and in society;
- to give the child a central position in the life of grown-ups;
- to promote – in a wider sense – the physical conditions in which children grow up;
- to promote equal opportunities, in the conditions of life of children, both in a material and in a cultural sense.

(Vilien 1993: 20)

However, despite the apparent differences in policy emphasis, UK and Scandinavian centres tended to make similar statements about their aims for children under 3. Some made reference to basic care while others gave emphasis to the environment and the programme. An amalgamation of Scandinavian comments suggests that they thought it was important that little by little children could learn to put clothes on and take them off unaided, and that in some way they should practise eating and going to the toilet. A safe and warm atmosphere was also considered important to their work; they wanted to support the 'being' of children. In addition, they wanted to offer to all children many-sided experiences in music, drawing and physical education. One of the most important aspects of their work seemed to be the development of social skills. They believed that these things helped the children to grow into balanced, independent people, who are eager to learn new things.

The Scandinavian centres emphasized the importance of an environment that was warm, with close relationships with other children and adults who would support individual children's development by offering regular programmes of short activities to develop concentration and confidence. It was believed that such programmes would increase children's self-confidence and emotional well-being.

Regular programmes, primary care, safety, a sense of security, a range of interesting and developing activities were all much the same as we found in the UK responses. However, some interesting differences emerged as to why such aims were held and how they were interpreted in practice. The following are some of the beliefs extracted from the Scandinavian questionnaires. They are listed as they were written in response to the research questionnaire:

These factors help the child to grow in a healthy way; to receive healthy and good self-esteem and have a happy childhood in day care.

- We want that each child should feel good enough.
- We don't teach the children but they learn by playful methods.
- We must read children's body language very well and make a good understanding of it.
- That every child should reach a maximum development in their own time. That every child gets a good self-respect and is accepted for what s/he is.

- That every child shall be able to develop good relations with both other children and adults.
- They'll feel confident in the group, take consideration and accept that we are all different and unique and help each other.
- . . . let them examine success . . . and let them try, try and try.
- Security, self-confidence and sociability. THE CHILD SHOULD FEEL 'GOOD ENOUGH'.
- Good relationships with the parents, a lot of tenderness and nearness. That children should have calm surroundings with toys that make it possible for them to discover and arouse their interest and curiosity.
- The programme for smaller children is more based on tenderness, nearness and confirmation.
- Together with parents, create harmonious children.
- The children must feel confidence, peacefulness and joy. We have to support the self-esteem. We help children how to feel responsibility.
- We want them to learn to respect each other and to be independent human beings.
- We want them to have positive feelings to be in a group . . . to care for each other.
- . . . give them activity which gives them mobility.
- We give a child a feeling of safety and warmth – these things are important for the beginning of life.
- We try to make them feel safe, that someone cares for them, we talk about feelings.
- We want the children to be safe and harmonious.
- Small children learn through their senses so we help them through feelings, tasting, exploring . . . little children need time, love and compassion.
- We listen to children very carefully and try to understand their thoughts.

A very particular ethos appeared to exist in the Scandinavian centres. The focus of the provision or programmes offered seemed to be centred upon an individualistic 'child development' approach: nurturing a sense of self in each child that they might grow and develop at their own rate and in their own direction. The adult role here is to 'be with' the child while this is happening and to respond to their understanding of the child's needs at any given moment. The childcare workers seemed to show a commitment to the importance of group support and community but felt that this came from unique and individual contributions.

The UK responses seem to be more ambivalent, possibly reflecting the tension between a pre-school education model of early years provision and a child development model. As Bennett (1992: 19) says:

For the English speaker, the term pre-school education will seem to channel the young child towards cognitive development and away from family, social and cultural experience which are the bedrock of human experience . . . the term early childhood development would seem to correspond more to contemporary understanding of how children develop and learn.

However, the context of educare in the UK means that educarers will probably be working with both models to some extent. My interest is in how, despite this difference in emphasis, educarers in the UK plan for and provide curricula that nurture children's sense of personal identity and self-worth.

How appropriate are our centre programmes and how do we define 'appropriate'? The following case studies are taken from my research in two quite different early years establishments in the North-West of England. They are offered as a stimulus for discussion, to raise questions and possibly to help give the reader an opportunity to rethink particular beliefs about the aims of educare for children under 3.

Case study 1 – children between 18 months and 30 months

It was 'circle time' and the children and staff were sitting on the floor, rolling a ball to each other, saying the name of the person they were rolling the ball to. Children had been asked to open their legs wide to catch the ball.

While this was happening a child arrived, somewhat distressed and clinging tightly to her mother, who stayed for a while until the child felt more at ease. Eventually a member of staff took the child on her knee to be involved in the play, which by this time was action rhymes.

Eventually the group was divided into two and one group left for another room (home base). The children who remained were asked 'Who would like to make a picture of mummy?' Eventually five children chose this activity (although it had been planned and prepared for four – a fifth set of materials was soon added). Other children moved to different activities around the room. The centre was celebrating International Women's Week, and this was to include the very youngest children.

Each child had a seat and access to their own selection of 'people', coloured papers and paints. The children were eager to start and all the time the adult was explaining the purpose of the activity.

Once the choices had been made and children were enjoying the experience of painting, the educarer began to raise questions about what their mothers did while 'we' were at the nursery.

Because the staff member knew a great deal about the children and their families she was able to help the children articulate their ideas and understanding, and so would prompt if appropriate.

Some of the comments the children made were: 'Mummy goes to school'; 'Mummy washes plates'; 'Mummy's at the hospital'; 'Mummy looks after my baby.'

At each opportunity the educarer extended the discussion, giving value to all that the children offered and to the work of the women, the children's mothers. She also talked about other things women did and pointed to photographs on the wall: 'Mummies can be firefighters and doctors and be police officers.'

The educarer encouraged the children to remember ideas and comments made earlier in circle time when they had talked about how hard it was to look after a baby. She talked to each child about the colour of the paint and paper they chose and how this reflected the colour of their mummy, again using a photograph exhibition on the wall. (The activity had been located carefully beside these displays.) The educarer modelled and talked through what the children were doing but only after each child had made their own attempt, and she continually reinforced the value of women's contributions.

Each picture was discussed in turn, and when two of the children wanted to produce another one that was encouraged. The pictures were the children's exploration of paint on paper and represented each child's level of interest and stage of development. They were later mounted and displayed alongside the photographs of each child's mother.

Later in the morning, story time gave an added opportunity to discuss the paintings and the earlier conversations. All the children enjoyed this activity. The pace was not hurried; the children were happy to talk about their 'mummy', showing a good deal of knowledge and having their attempts at descriptions supported and developed.

In my discussion with the educarer later that day she made a self-evaluation and presented me with her rationale. She talked about the importance of her voice, the tone and pitch of it and of how she created intimacy and therefore the opportunity for trust and self-confidence in the children by a closeness, moving in toward children as they spoke and giving full attention to the speaking child but still finding physical ways of involving the other children in what was happening or being said. She felt her eye movements and facial expressions showed interest and enjoyment in what children were saying and were a way of prompting children to continue without verbal requests. She used other prompting techniques to aid children's memories and recall abilities. She knew each child very well via the key worker system and so had much of the missing information when the children didn't know what mummy did or where she was. She encouraged the children to talk to each other by creating a discussion rather than a question-and-answer session. By speaking to the children in a conversational voice rather than a directive or patronizing one, by exploring ideas together rather than just explaining, by using the correct terminology and if necessary by following this with some reinforcement of understanding: through all of these methods she was showing respect, interest, encouragement and recognizing and promoting individuality in the children, most importantly by doing all of this in a sincere and honest way, genuinely enjoying the contributions of each child.

There were no demands made upon the parent to leave a distressed child, nor upon the child to leave the parent before she was ready. The time, space and respect needed was allowed and encouraged. Joining an established group can be traumatic for children in the same way it can be for adults; the staff's gentle handling of the situation showed the importance they attached to how each child might feel about their arrival at the centre.

When the fifth set of art materials was produced, in recognition of a child's desire to be involved with the planned activity, it was evident that the centre worker wished to respond positively and immediately and to capitalize on that moment in time and the enthusiasm the child brought with him. There was no expectation that the child should wait and perhaps become frustrated, disruptive or lose interest.

Case study 2 – children between 6 months and 18 months

A and C (nursery officers) were responsible for five children at the time of the observation. The children who had been sleeping were beginning to wake.

T was the first to stir and his mood was happy. C lifted him from his bed, talking calmly and softly to him, welcoming him back to play. One by one each of the children began to wake. The response was always the same from the nursery officers – always reassuring and warm. Some of the children required longer than others to recover full consciousness; these children were held closely and accompanied A and C as they responded to other children.

Most of the children were able to walk; as they came round they moved to what interested them. The immobile children were placed near activities the staff knew they enjoyed and somehow all the children were happily awake and playing within 15 minutes. The two educarers were at all times completely involved with the children – talking, singing, playing with them or holding, cuddling them. Children were changed from wet to dry pants/nappies easily and comfortably. None of the children objected, perhaps because of the gentle and/or fun way the task was performed (it was a different experience for each child).

B, who likes to climb onto chairs and tables, had the watchful eye of C at all times whatever else she was doing. When she anticipated the risk of a fall she positioned herself close by, not to prevent an experience for B but to ensure her safety. Occasionally this meant catching a falling B!

In my later discussion with A and C they talked about the enjoyment they found in caring for these very young children and how aware they were of the different natures and personalities of each child. C, in particular, felt that the rapid growth that occurs in these early stages was a rewarding experience to witness. To be involved with children discovering what they could do, and to have the responsibility of ensuring they have the opportunity to try lots of different things gave C a great deal of personal and professional satisfaction. Both of the nursery officers were very confident in their ability to respond differently to each child and to recognize and value each as different. A and C believed they were protecting the self-esteem of the children in their care while promoting their self-image.

The three educarers in both the case studies were mature and experienced. While they had a great deal of autonomy in the provision they made there were many influences and expectations at play. All three were trained nursery nurses; prior to their current post each had various forms of employment with young children, such as nanny, day nursery officer, family centre worker, nursery class assistant. Two of the three were parents. None was currently involved with a continuing professional development programme but all had access to, and had availed themselves of, short, post-qualifying training courses. Case study 1 was in a local education authority children's centre while Case study 2 was in an independent day nursery.

Both the studies gave supporting evidence to the original comments made in the questionnaire (which had been completed prior to my observation visits). The approaches made to children both physically and emotionally were gentle and positive. There were opportunities for children to choose *not* to become involved with what was offered as well as to continue for longer than planned. Although in both cases the adults had selected the materials and equipment and therefore set the agenda, the children's interest and happiness were sustained by the skilful interactions of the adults and their knowledge of the children and their families.

Both case studies are offered as examples of the adults' interpretation of 'appropriate programmes' in terms of supporting the individuality of the child by valuing cultural heritage, extending knowledge and understanding, emphasizing the uniqueness of individuals and families and by having a warm, close and tactile relationship with each child. Mirrors, photographs and artwork in both centres were deliberately used as an instrument of self-awareness.

My view is that both these case studies show educarers working sensitively with children's self-image and esteem. The terms 'self-image' and 'self-esteem' are sometimes mistakenly used interchangeably: 'Self-esteem is to possess a favourable opinion of oneself, while image is defined as likeness, symbol, mental picture or the reliving of a sensation in the absence of the original stimulus' (Kunjufu 1984: 15).

Kunjufu suggests that self-imagery could be viewed as a process which affects self-esteem. If this is the case, and if we consider self-esteem or feeling good about oneself to be a valuable possession, then where is the heading 'self-image' in our early childhood programmes, in our curricula, in our activities or play plans for our youngest children, who are embarked upon a voyage of discovery that will tell them who they are and what they can achieve?

From the very moment of birth we are all engaged in a process of becoming 'ourselves'. It no doubt takes a lifetime to complete the picture. However, those early foundations laid by our primary caregivers (and those caregivers they trust to continue the work) are crucial to the picture we paint of ourselves. Closely linked to the way we view ourselves is the way we think other people see us: 'If childcare workers understand the importance of having a positive self-image and the need to value themselves (self-esteem) they are more likely to develop self-esteem in children' (Beaver *et al.* 1994: 174).

There have been many writers, researchers and colleagues who at various points and in a whole range of ways have influenced my thinking in my current attempt to uncover what might be happening to the self-image of young children in group settings.

One particular document and its underpinning philosophy has had a powerful effect upon my vision and has strongly influenced the direction I have taken in my research.

The Draft Guidelines for Developmentally Appropriate Programmes for Early Childhood Services produced for the Ministry of Education, New Zealand and called *Te Whariki* were informed by the following aspirations

for children: 'To grow up as competent and confident learners and commu-
nicators, healthy in mind, body, spirit, secure in their sense of belonging and
in the knowledge that they make a valued contribution to society' (MoE
1993: 8).

The Curriculum Whariki (mat) is seen as a weaving together of principles
and aims in order to meet those aspirations:

Principles
Empowerment
Holistic development
Family and community
Relationships

Aims
Well-being
Belonging
Contribution
Communication
Exploration

As the principles and aims are skilfully woven together by the many practitioners in a range and variety of settings, each mat will be differently
unique to a community, but children will experience the Curriculum
Whariki.

Can you see 'self-image' as a priority woven in with these principles or
aims? Is it woven into the programme you offer? I could see it woven into
much of the practice in the two centres where I did my research.

Over a period of months, my observations and discussions with the staff at
both centres, coupled with my empathy and alignment to the curriculum Te
Whariki, led me to develop some headings in order to focus further discussion. I asked staff to think, write and/or talk about how they ensure that children have the opportunity to experience:

- dignity and autonomy,
- esteem as an individual,
- spontaneous expression,
- independent thought,
- respect for their rights as defined by the United Nations Convention
  (Rights for Us Group 1994),
- self-confidence,
- a sense of belonging.

The responses varied, thus perhaps demonstrating the range and levels of
understanding: some of the staff were young and inexperienced and tended
to quote text they remembered from their studies; other more experienced
staff used examples of practice to highlight their thoughts; and a smaller
number talked in philosophical or ideological terms.

Dignity and autonomy

There was a very strong view that adults must keep in mind children's feelings and opinions when performing routines and activities. This would include showing respect for privacy when changing or toileting a child. This was demonstrated in Case study 1 (the unhappy child joining the group and the level of control the children had in the painting activity) and in Case study 2, where there was substantial evidence of sensitivity to how each child felt when they awoke.

Staff emphasized the importance of each child by encouraging children to 'push' themselves and by showing each child how their contribution was valued in calm and genuine ways. Staff believed it to be vital to recognize when there is no 'active' role for the adult in a child's play (both centres used treasure baskets/heuristic play allowing total freedom and autonomy) (Goldschmied and Jackson 1994: 118). There was a need to be a 'playmate' when invited to respond rather than to initiate activities. They also thought it important to keep equipment at a level where children can help themselves and make their own selection, with the adult role to ensure the safety of the activity and the environment. Involving children in setting out activities, preparation for routines, lunch, etc.; encouraging decision making about what they want to eat, how much, when they want a drink or to go outside; helping children to deal with conflict rather than doing it for them – all were considered to be real ways of ensuring each child had the opportunity to experience dignity and autonomy.

Staff in the two centres felt strongly about unnecessary interruptions to the flow of a child's play for the sake of routines. Most staff believed it imperative to discuss changes (staff absences, new routines) with children, to offer reasons, explanations and support.

Esteem as an individual

The comments from staff in both centres on this subject were clear and made with conviction. The need for children to be valued for who they are was uniformly expressed and manifested in each case study. As one educarer in Case study 1 said, 'The need to give praise and recognition for each child's attempt rather than achievements, the encouragement to try new things and to enjoy their creations and ideas with each other'.

By beginning each day positively and being happy to see/receive them into the centre, by having strong relationships with parents, you can encourage trust, honesty and security with children. By being interested and involved with a child, showing care and attention to what they do and listening to what they have to say and by showing trust, confidence and encouraging responsibility and high self-expectation, each child will have the opportunity to experience a view of themselves constructed as a result of positive, individualistic, personal and intimate interaction.

Although it was not always possible, staff were aware that routines and schedules should be about children's needs rather than adults'.

Spontaneous expression

Unless spontaneity is damaged, as in the case of Alex, young children will freely express how they feel. In practice, how best to encourage this natural direction and how to aid a child's ability to manage this was felt to be quite a complex question. It was, however, high on the agenda in both centres and is evident in the case studies.

Examples of how it might be achieved were considered to be:

- offering lots of opportunity for imaginative play;
- encouraging talk and giving children the language they might need for this;
- encouraging laughter and sharing it;
- creating opportunities for children to release feelings safely by having 'noise making' areas;
- sharing your feelings with children;
- recognizing and developing your own body language and learning to understand that of individual children;
- giving encouragement by smiling, touching, using physical movements, keeping questions open and allowing children time to formulate their responses;
- having music available for playing, dancing, listening to, enjoying;
- encouraging dramatic play with stories;
- having lots of creative material available to try things out, make things, etc. and valuing children's creations (it is does not necessarily mean displaying them – allow the child to decide what should happen to their own creation (Griffin 1994: 175));
- being sensitive to changes in behaviour (find out why!) and give children feedback (we all need this!).

Independent thought

Children's ideas might be limited by the access they have to materials – can the possibilities be widened? Try to remove the barriers to children acting upon their thoughts. This might be a gate to the toilet area or to an outside space – question yourself, does it need to be there? Encourage decision making in children and provide the real opportunities for this to happen often. Talk children through their actions: this should include possible consequences – get children to predict these. Encourage group activities, teamwork where cooperation brings obvious success (this is only possible where individual children are able to cooperate; experience of the process can be encouraged, however). Develop group problem solving activities: these should be real and not abstract, i.e. the sharing of fruit, or what we might need before we go outside, etc. Ask children's opinions – encourage them to have one! Talk to children in conflict and encourage them to reach agreement. Use stories (not always from books) and encourage the child to develop or to change a familiar story. Offer plenty of choice of activity, materials or the location of where the play might happen; draw out the child's ideas and where possible, put these ideas into action. Always respond to requests, even if the answer is 'no' – then give reasons. Provide heuristic play opportunities, puzzles and guessing games.

Respect for children's rights

Staff in the research sites had varying knowledge of the 1989 United Nations Convention on the Rights of the Child. They were, however, very aware that children have human rights by definition; as a consequence they should be treated at all times with this in mind. Staff were able to comment upon their strategies for implementing this ideal. There are many examples of their views in practice, highlighted within both case studies.

Children should be encouraged to express their needs and wishes and be given the language to do so where necessary. Children should be encouraged and not pressured into things; respect should be shown to a child's right to be upset, hurt or angry. Staff were very aware of their own vulnerability at times of personal difficulty and how it was necessary to guard against this having an effect upon the ways in which they might handle a child. The giving of explanations commensurate with a child's understanding seemed to be significant to all who participated. For some this meant using simple language, for others it was a much more complex issue of the right to access information. All believed children have the right to choose not to do things or to try to do things they couldn't do at an earlier point. Both centres believed they recognized and valued differences and that children had a right to have that difference valued (Article 2). This was so expertly shown in Case study 1 when children of different races and cultures were exploring, examining and celebrating themselves and their mothers (Article 8 and 30).

Childhood is a once-only experience and professionals should remember that children have a right to a happy one when they are planning how children's time will be spent. Caring and knowledgeable adults might both improve respect for children's rights and help children learn about those rights.

Self-confidence

The research showed that staff believed that the celebration of what children *can do* was the cornerstone of this topic. Educarers should provide a secure environment where children have the courage to attempt new things and are given the time, interest and positive responses from adults who have ensured that the environment offers safe but challenging opportunities. In these circumstances children will not only learn what they can do but will know it is safe and all right to keep on finding out what more they can do. Case study 2 shows how an experienced and aware member of staff supported the development of a child who was secure in the knowledge that he could climb on, up and over all the fixtures in the nursery room. By giving children the chance to take one more step up the stair, along the climbing frame – or for babies, the great distance between one piece of equipment/furniture and another – we will be creating the climate for courage to grow. Staff felt that children needed to be happy being where they were and who they were with, because being relaxed comes before being brave. It was considered important to encourage older toddlers to care for younger babies and that by sharing toys, ideas and play, children become more confident in what they do and give. Children are encouraged to talk about home and what they do there; to assist each other with coats, aprons and tissues; and to comfort others when they are upset. When offering socio-dramatic play, one must ensure enough materials are available: young children might find it difficult to wait – this is particularly important for children who have not yet begun to share. Children can take responsibility for tidying up alongside an adult. Dancing, singing, telling news and stories all help children to feel confident about who they are and what they can do. By giving very individual attention to a child, based upon sound knowledge, understanding and affection, the power to feel good about who you are and what you can do will be nurtured.

A sense of belonging

It was in this section that the key worker system was given most consideration. Both sites operated the system, though they differed in their understanding of and commitment to it. It was most strongly demonstrated in the nursery where Case study 2 was observed.

Developing a close and honest relationship with children and their parents requires time to get to know about each other and to learn to trust and depend upon each other. One of the centres offers a two-person system. Here two members of staff work closely together to offer continuity throughout breaks, holidays and shifts. Both operate a daily diary in which parents and staff pass on information. The need to work collaboratively establishes, if not ensures, the potential for continuity between home and centre. Sleeping locations and positions could be static and offer a similar experience to one that a child might have at home; a teddy, dummy or a blanket from home could be brought in.

Other helpful measures could be:

- allowing children to have their own drawer or box in which to keep whatever they wish and to have their own space/area for clothes and toiletries (this might be reinforced with photographs);
- having a gradual admissions policy and settling-in period when a child can get to know who the other people are in the rooms, and become comfortable in that knowledge;
- having times when 'family groups' (a group of children with the same key worker) do things exclusively together (Case study 1): this would certainly include meal times but could also mean going outside to play together, or baking;
- holding regular team/staff meetings to ensure that all staff have some knowledge of all the children;
- having the same one or two people meet the child's needs wherever possible and not rushing children through routines (Case study 2);
- feeding, changing, etc. but using these times as an opportunity to develop an even closer relationship;

- giving children clear and realistic boundaries and remaining consistent (it is important that this is in collaboration with families) and that any criticism of a child's behaviour is directed at the action and not at the child;
- giving and receiving warm cuddles and being happy to share your days with each child.

These comments do not form an exhaustive list but do represent the ideas of those consulted; they give a flavour of much of the practice observed on my study visits. The views expressed, I believe, link very closely to the case studies.

As shown in Case study 1, the adult used her in-depth knowledge of each child in order to encourage them to talk about mummy and to choose accurate skin colour and to think about what mummy does. The way she responded to a distressed child and to an eager one who wished to be part of the activity are examples of educarers' views of good practice. Her knowledge came from a trusting relationship with children and families developed through time. She was fully committed to and understood the importance of building this kind of relationship. The recognition of the value of each child's race, culture and contribution came from a commitment to the celebration of difference. Her responses to distressed or eager children were an acknowledgement of, and respect for, children's feelings.

Case study 2 demonstrates how sensitive, knowledgeable adults can skilfully adapt their actions and responses to the different needs and personality of each child while acknowledging her entitlement to be recognized as a unique individual.

I am now going to explore briefly the parental perspective. Valuing children means valuing families; to have consulted staff alone would have limited any findings and/or interpretations to a professional perspective. Thus the following remarks are included to show how parents perceived the needs of their children in early years settings, and on what basis they arrived at their judgements.

Parents' concerns

The major concern of all the parents I talked to was the happiness of their child; this came before curriculum content, staff:child ratios or training and qualifications held by staff.

All felt it was important that staff enjoyed 'my child'. Value was given to the willingness of staff to chat to parents about the day's events: 'how well they know the children. I feel this approach is a good illustration of their professional shared-care approach which I find very reassuring.'

The regular informal discussion, in addition to the more formal timetabled events, confirmed to parents that staff knew, understood and cared for each child. Parents wanted staff to have a strong bond with their child, to offer care as a mother would and felt that the key worker system serviced this very well – 'She is as proud of his achievements as I am.' Several parents used the word 'trust': 'My child trusts the staff here so of course I do.'

All parents believed their child enjoyed the nursery (both sites) and would talk freely about people and events and of how the staff were missed at week-ends, so close were the relationships. Parents were aware that their child had developed in skills, knowledge and ability. However, most significantly and commonly referred to was the growth in confidence in every case. The atmosphere of the nursery was discussed in some detail in terms of 'happy', 'warm' and 'friendly'. Parents were very pleased with the environment and recognized the teamwork which contributed to this: 'There are always plenty of staff about, helping each other, plenty of capable hands.'

It was clearly of prime importance to parents that each child had a positive and strong bond with at least one other adult and that this adult would have genuine affection, interest and involvement with that child; parents hoped their child's educarer would want and expect the best for them in the same way that a parent would.

In discussions about what parents wanted their children to gain from the nursery experience there were again common themes. Discussion centred around confidence, independence and sociability.

- I want him to feel good about himself.
- When I was looking for a nursery I watched the staff and how they interacted with children. I looked for happy children.
- I want her to gain confidence.
- . . . that he feels good about himself.
- His confidence has grown so rapidly he is a very assured child now.
- Mostly I want him to gain in independence and be a happy sociable child.
- . . . that the children are happy.
- It's important that the staff encourage children to be independent but that they also encourage sociability.

The parents I consulted were very aware of the importance of their children's emotional health and how it was inextricably linked to the relationship with their educarer. It seems to me that human relationship is the most significant issue for parents when they are entrusting their children's most formative years to the care of others. While both case studies suggest that for the adults involved in the two centres this also was a priority, it begs the question: is this always the case?

Looking back to the extracts from the UK responses to the questionnaire, they suggest there may be other influences at play.

Issues for further consideration

De Jonckheere and Griffin (1994), in an attempt to provide guidance for educarers in their search for quality of experience for children under 3, raise the following questions:

- Do the adults involved with the children recognize their rights?
- Does the service offer education and care (educare) to all the children irrespective of their age?
- Does the management team recognize the need for, and encourage, continuing staff development and training?

- Does the management team hold high expectations of themselves and others?
- Do staff take part in regular and continuing multidisciplinary training?
- Do staff have the ability to follow a child-led agenda?
- Are all adults involved in the child's educare work in genuine partnership with one another so that they can best meet the changing needs of both the individual child and her family?

In addition to these questions, I would add further indicators that have emerged from this study which may be helpful in trying to understand how best we might provide for our youngest and most vulnerable children. These include the following:

- Staff must enjoy working with this age group and be able to respond positively in very physical ways.
- The best consistency and continuity of care comes from a genuine relationship with parents and carers, one that stimulates ongoing, in-depth discussion.
- There should be recognition that the child's known environment and primary caregiver has changed. Hence as much else as is possible needs to continue to be the same: sleep patterns, eating habits, comforters, etc. in order to respond to the child as an individual.
- All planning and preparation for the child's day should be focused on the known interests and needs of each individual child.
- The child's happiness is the prime consideration at all times.
- Safety issues are the adults' concern and should not be used as a rationale for not allowing children freedom of expression or choice of activity.
- Expectations of children should be related to knowledge of the child and the ability to read clues, i.e. body language, early verbalization, crying, first steps – not predetermined checklists.
- Adult involvement in a child's play should be at that child's level, preserving the child's spontaneity.
- Children's self-confidence should be encouraged by valuing the child, not what they have achieved.

Some conclusions

I have discussed in some detail several approaches to making provision for young children in the UK and Scandinavia. I hope I have given some opportunity for the reader to respond and to raise some questions. By focusing programmes upon predetermined ideals and establishing a hierarchy for young children to attain, we may risk losing the wonderful world that is the inner being of that individual, the uniqueness of that child that has never before existed nor will ever again, and only can because that child exists. 'Have we in our education system really put emphasis on human values? Or have we been so blinded by material rewards that we have failed to recognize that the real values of a democracy lie in its most precious asset, the individual?' (Lowenfeld and Brittain 1987: 2). We may place in jeopardy all that child brings with her to our world which will touch it, and perhaps change it. We

may endanger a whole generation of children who have rights and expectations and who place in our hands their today and their tomorrow. We should
not treat this lightly.

The first year in human life is the year when you learn the most.
The second year in human life is the year when you learn next most.
The third year in human life is the year when you learn third most.

(Larsen 1992: 150)

References

Abbott, L. and Gillen, J. (1997) *Educare for the Under Threes – Identifying Need and
Opportunity.* Report of the research study by the Manchester Metropolitan
University jointly funded with the Esmée Fairbairn Charitable Trust. Man-
chester: The Manchester Metropolitan University.
Beaver, M., Brewster, J., Jones, P., Keene, A., Neaum, S. and Tallack, J. (1994) *Babies
and Young Children. Book 1: Development 0–7.* Cheltenham: Stanley Thorne.
Bennett, J. (1992) *Early Childhood Intervention: An Overview of Practice North and
South in Educare in Europe,* Report of the European Childcare Conference,
Copenhagen. Paris: UNESCO.
Bergman, M. (1993) Early childhood care in education in Sweden, in T. David
(ed.) *Educational Provision for Our Youngest Children: A European Perspective.*
London: Paul Chapman Publishing.
De Jonckheere, S. and Griffin, B. (1994) Educare for under threes, in R. Rodger
(ed.) *An Identification of Factors Contributing to Quality Educare for Children under
Five,* Research project. Manchester: The Manchester Metropolitan University.
Goldschmied, E. and Jackson, S. (1994) *People Under Three – Young Children in Day
Care.* London: Routledge.
Griffin, B. (1994) 'Look at me – I'm only two': educare for under threes, in L.
Abbott and R. Rodger (eds) *Quality Education in the Early Years.* Buckingham:
Open University Press.
Kunjufu, J. (1984) *Developing Positive Self-Images and Discipline in Black Children.*
Chicago: African American Images.
Larsen, S. (1992) *Epilogue in Educare in Europe,* Conference report, The Royal
Danish School of Education Studies, The Board of Directors of the Danish Col-
leges for Pre-School and Social Care Teacher Training, The Danish National
Federation of Early Childhood and Youth Education and the Danish National
Commission for UNESCO.
Lowenfeld, V. and Brittain, W. L. (1987) *Creative and Mental Growth,* 8th edn. New
York: Macmillan.
Marsh, C. (1997) 'They're always happy to chat about any problems you have' –
how educators develop relationships with parents and children, in L. Abbott
and H. Moylett (eds) *Working with the Under-threes: Training and Professional
Development.* Buckingham: Open University Press.
Ministry of Education [MoE] (1993) *Te Whariki.* Wellington, New Zealand:
Learning Media.
Rights for Us Group (1994) *A Guide to Rights: By Young People for Young People from
the United Nations Convention.* London: Save the Children.
Vilien, K. (1993) Provision for pre-school children in Denmark, in T. David (ed.)
Education Provision for Children: European Perspectives. London: Paul Chapman
Publishing.

3 | 'This says "Happy New Year"' – learning to be literate: reading and writing with young children

Caroline Barratt-Pugh

In the early 1970s, when I first started work as a nursery nurse, I arrived at the day care centre with a bundle of labels all ready to place around the room. Then I noticed the following letter pinned to the staff information board. It stated that:

> Writing in any form must not be displayed, this includes captions under children's pictures and labels. Books must not be freely available in the Centre and only used by responsible adults. Young children are not ready to learn to read or write, and any materials related to these areas are inappropriate and can cause anxiety and confusion.

Well, things have certainly changed since then, not only in relation to decision making processes, but also in relation to beliefs about literacy.

During the past 25 years my understanding and experience of literacy development has undergone a number of radical changes, through which all the children I have worked with have survived and even flourished! At the beginning of my teaching career in the 1970s I remember a number of pre-primary programmes, set up in order to prepare children for formal reading instruction when they entered school. It was believed that children had to be 'ready' to read and had to be 'taught' how to read through direct and systematic instruction (Crawford 1995). Developmental readiness could be enhanced through visual discrimination activities; identification of colours, shapes numbers and letters; left to right progression; and sound-letter correspondence (Teale and Sulzby 1986). Children from particular social, economic and cultural backgrounds were identified as 'disadvantaged' and placed in special programmes such as 'Head Start' and 'HighScope'. Thus family and community literacy practices were not acknowledged and any form of reading and writing was seen as inappropriate for young children, in formal care and education contexts.

As children reached a particular developmental stage it was believed they were ready to begin formal reading and writing instruction. As a classroom teacher in the late 1970s it was my job to teach a clearly identified set of hier-archical formal reading skills. Reading and writing were seen as quite sep-arate. Writing consisted largely of copying patterns, which led to copying sentences, which were constructed by the teacher. However, by the early 1980s, Jayne (one of my 5-year-olds) seemed to suggest that reading could be more than repetition of the alphabetic code, memorizing decontextualized words and learning a series of isolated skills: she cut up her box of 'Words I know', stuck them on her Mother's Day card and claimed that she could now read and write!

During the time I was lecturing in early childhood education at the Man-chester Metropolitan University, a number of alternative perspectives on early literacy emerged. Two current perspectives grew from research into family and community literacy practices. These are known as *emergent lit-eracy* perspectives and *social constructivist* perspectives. Within each of these views it is argued that children begin to develop literacy almost from birth, through their interaction with others, in a range of social and cultural events. Each perspective emphasizes the importance of authentic reading and writing activities, and stresses the need to build on children's under-standings about literacy when planning programmes in care and educa-tional settings. Although these perspectives differ in their view of the processes involved in the development of literacy, they agree that in order to plan effective literacy environments, carers need to start by looking at what children in their care know about literacy.

My current research in Western Australia, where I work in the School of Language and Literacy, at Edith Cowan University, Perth, is concerned with the relationship between home and school literacy practices. Through this research I have become increasingly interested in the ways in which young children become literate, and the role of formal care and educational institu-tions in literacy learning. In order to explore the role of the family and com-munity in early literacy development, and the ways in which educare workers can build on and extend children's pre-existing knowledge and skills, in this chapter I am going to address the following questions:

- What do young children know about literacy?
- How can this knowledge of literacy be supported and enhanced?
- Where to next? Conclusions and questions.

Let us explore these questions through observation and analysis of young children engaged in literacy practices in a community family day care centre. The analysis will raise some interesting issues and lead to a number of ques-tions about literacy in the early years

Inside a community family day care centre

Imagine you have been invited to spend a day at a local community family day care centre, observing the under-threes. You are particularly interested in literacy. It's 7.30 a.m., you have just arrived, and as you enter the centre you are immediately struck by a giant-size poster with the words 'Welcome to our centre' written in a variety of different languages. The director of the centre greets you and begins to show you around. You cannot help but notice the aroma of freshly baked bread. The director explains that each week parents or guardians are invited to bring in simple recipes for the kitchen staff to try. Today they are baking stollen, a German bread. The recipes are pinned to a board in the eating area and at the end of each month they are made into a booklet and sold. As you continue down the corridor you notice a variety of posters and notices along the wall. There is printed information with the following headings: 'The centre routine', 'Our programme' and colourful posters depicting beliefs about 'Our children' and 'The importance of play'. There are mobiles made by the children hanging from the ceiling, which partially hide the sign at the end of the corridor: 'Babies and toddlers – please close the door'.

Once inside the under-threes' room you make yourself comfortable and begin to look around. The room consists of a large central area surrounded by smaller 'cosy' spaces, with a reading corner within an area called 'Our book shop', a home corner and a huge home-made 'grotto' with 'Teddy Bears Picnic' painted on the entrance. There are two smaller semi-open-plan areas, one for changing and toileting and the other for preparing feeds. An open door leads into a room with cots and bedding. Some children have been here since 7.00 a.m. and are beginning to demand attention. You start to make notes as you observe the children around the room, focusing particularly on the literacy practices the babies and toddlers are involved in.

What do young children know about literacy?

Jane aged 24 months, is sitting in her cot holding a book called *Our Favourite Animals*. She is turning the pages backwards and forwards, looking intently at the pictures and whispering to herself. She points at several pictures and repeats: 'Putty cat, putty cat, wabbit, goggy . . . goggy'. On the next page, she softly calls out random numbers and begins to make a hooting sound followed by the words: 'hoot, hoot, hoot, hoot'.

Ishmael, 9 months old, is propped up on soft cushions in the book corner, surrounded by low shelves with a variety of books. He struggles to turn the pages of a small board book, but squeals with delight as he appears to recognize some of the brightly coloured illustrations, muttering, 'nana, nana' and 'dink' as he comes across bananas and a bottle of milk.

Ibrahim and Abdul, 34 months, Ishmael's older twin brothers are kneeling on the rug in the house corner. They are gently rocking backwards and forwards, with their hands together, softly chanting in Arabic. Later, Ibrahim reads *Where's Spot?* by covering up the words and proudly announcing, 'I know, no look!'

Masa, 27 months, and Susan, 30 months, are huddled together under a blanket, looking at *How the Birds Got their Colours* (Lofts 1983). The book is based on a story told by Mary Albert of the Bardi tribe to Aboriginal children living in Broome, Western Australia. The illustrations are based on children's paintings. Masa is telling the story and occasionally Susan joins in. Masa reads the phrases: 'Some got red, some brown, some blue, some yellow' while pointing at each illustration. Susan appears to be enthralled and gasps with delight as more birds appear, repeating after Masa, 'Some got spots. Some got stripes.' Suddenly, Susan demands that they go back, as Masa has turned several pages at once. An argument follows and as Masa tries to turn more pages and finish the story, Susan begins to cry.

Mei is 3 years old. She has brought a piece of writing by her sister, who is in Year 1 of the local Cambodian bilingual programme. She sits in the 'Art gallery' and begins to make marks around and on top of the Khmer script. At one point, Mei appears to copy with great care parts of the Khmer script. As she writes, she assigns a Khmer word to each mark or group of marks and continually repeats and points to each 'word'. Some of her independent marks appear to represent the Khmer script.

The carer draws your attention to Daniel who is almost 1 year old. He is sitting on Chantee's knee. Chantee, his sister, is in Year 2 of the Cambodian bilingual programme. As Daniel begins to stir and become fretful, Chantee sings a variety of rhymes in Khmer. She expertly engages Daniel in various moves and actions, capturing his attention and soothing him. Chantee appears to have an endless supply of rhymes and songs and alternates between English and Khmer.

What do these snapshots reveal about the children and their understanding of literacy?

Jane has brought *Our Favourite Animals* from home. She uses the actions modelled by her mum and grandma. She is beginning to learn that print is constant and that words have meaning which may be related to illustrations. She recognizes the difference between letters and numbers and she knows that words can represent the sounds animals make as she reads 'hoot, hoot'. She constantly returns to previous pages, as if checking her assumptions about some aspect of the book.

Although Ishmael is only 9 months old, he already seems to delight in the book he is handling. He recognizes that symbols represent objects and that objects have names. He is beginning to develop a curiosity about books as his interest in the world around him expands. Actually managing the book as well as looking at the pictures is quite an achievement for him.

Ibrahim and Abdul may be carrying out a practice that comes from their involvement in (or observation of) Islam, the religion within their home and community. The reciting of the Qur'an plays a significant part of their everyday lives. Progression through the Qur'an is seen as a great achievement by the family, and their older brother has just celebrated moving up to another level in the Qur'an. They are learning that literacy is a powerful and important part of religion, that literacy practices can take place within a shared and public activity, and that they can bring spiritual and social rewards. In addition, Ibrahim's comment about reading *Spot* suggests that he is learning that some reading involves repetition and memory.

Masa sweeps her finger under the words as she repeats the memorized sentences in *How the Birds Got their Colours* (Lofts 1983). She knows that her words are related to the print. She knows that print and pictures are different. She hesitates each time a new animal appears, and points to the picture. She knows that clues to meaning may be found in illustrations. Masa does not appear to be concerned about missing a few pages. Why does Susan become so upset? Perhaps she recognizes that narratives have sequences and that sequence may be important in maintaining meaning. Perhaps her familiarity with the book makes any disruption of the text distressing; is there some security in consistency? Perhaps her enjoyment of the story is spoilt when her expectations are not met. Whatever the reason, Susan's view of how this literacy practice should be carried out in this context have been challenged. She has already formed a clear idea of how story reading should be done.

Mei seems to be developing a sense of print orientation in Khmer. She writes from left to right and top to bottom and does not leave spaces between words (as is conventional in Khmer). Her marks show elements of the Khmer script. She relates random words to marks and seems to play a game of repetition, perhaps copying her sister's method of visual memorization. She knows that literacy can be done at home and at school, and that copying helps you to form letters correctly. She feels that her older sister can help her to write.

Daniel and Chantee are immersed in a rich oral culture at home. There are few books at home and their father emphasizes the importance of play. Oracy is central to the bilingual programme that Chantee attends. Chantee uses her expertise to calm and entertain Daniel. Chantee is helping Daniel to develop his knowledge and use of two languages simultaneously, as she occasionally sings a song in English. She is also immersing Daniel in cultural traditions and folklore. Although you can see that Chantee is facilitating Daniel's oral language development, as you finish your notes you wonder what this type of interaction has got to do with literacy development.

What does the above analysis tell us about learning literacy?

Firstly, regardless of their age all the children described above know something about literacy. During the past 15 or so years there have been numerous studies which suggest that literacy development begins at birth. Some of the children are developing literacy in more than one language, they are becoming biliterate. It is argued that children who grow up in print-orientated societies begin, at a very early age, to experiment with and hypothesize about the nature of print. In other words, young children try to make sense of the print that surrounds them. They become engaged in discovering the functions of print and working out the symbolic nature of print. Thus children play an active role in coming to understand and use literacy (Hiebert 1978; Taylor 1983; Teale and Sulzby 1986; Strickland and Morrow 1989; Miller 1996). This particular view of literacy is often referred to as *emergent literacy*, in which children's literacy learning is characterized by a progression through a series of developmental stages.

Secondly, it seems that the children are developing different kinds of knowledge about what literacy can be used for and how it is 'done'. This is not just a question of maturity or developmental stage. Rather, it is argued that literacy is more than cognitive achievements by the child, is based on the child's 'participation in culturally defined structures of knowledge and communication' (Snow *et al.* 1991: 175). That is, each child is learning about literacy through their involvement in social and cultural practices, which begins in early childhood. As with emergent literacy, children are seen as active participants in the exploration and understanding of print and literacy is learned through authentic engagement with a variety of texts. However, rather than conceptualizing children as progressing through a series of stages it is considered that they 'engage in the same types of literacy processes, though at a less sophisticated level, as those engaged in by older children and adults' (Crawford 1995: 81). This perspective is referred to as the *social constructivist* theory (Harste *et al.* 1984; Newkirk 1989).

Thirdly, the children are learning about what counts as literacy and how literacy is 'done' through the activities they are involved in: at home, within the community and at the community family centre. Anstey and Bull (1996: 152) suggest that 'an individual learns to behave in certain ways in literacy events and learns a number of particular literacy practices which are representative of his or her social and cultural groups'. Each activity that involves literacy consists of goals, rules for participation, and ways of carrying out the activity. These vary according to the social and cultural context in which they occur. For example, purposes for reading, writing and viewing will determine the way these are carried out in different family and community settings. Thus what Ibrahim and Abdul know about and can do with literacy may differ considerably from Masa's understanding and practices. These, in turn, may diverge from those literacy practices children encounter in the more formal setting of the family centre. This concept of literacy brings into play the notion of power and raises the following questions. Are some literacy practices valued more than others? Do some cultural groups have their literacy practices endorsed while others are ignored or made to restructure their practices? If this is true, do some children become empowered while others are constrained? This view of literacy builds on social constructivist theory and has been identified as a *critical* perspective (Solsken 1993; Luke 1994).

Fourthly, oral language seems to be an integral part of the children's literacy activities. Masa and Susan argue about how the story should be read. Jane differentiates between the sounds the owl makes and the written representation of that sound. Ishmael shouts with delight as he recognizes objects, and Mei repeats the words she has written over and over again. Ibrahim and Abdul see reciting Arabic out loud, from memory, as one of the main goals of the activity. These examples suggest that literacy and oracy are interrelated in two ways. Oracy can be an integral part of carrying out the literacy activity (as with Ibrahim, Abdul and Mei) and it can be a way of sharing, negotiating and promoting both meaning and literacy procedures. Thus oracy seems to be an important part of learning to be literate.

Fifthly, literacy takes many forms. Recent research suggests that 'certain kinds of oral behaviours utilise the same kinds of strategies or ways of thinking about or responding to text that are found in literacy. These strategies include sequencing, explaining, evaluating, elaborating and clarifying, arguing, persuading, responding and analysing' (Hudelson 1994: 139–40). Reporting on an ongoing research project Hudelson (1994) has found a relationship between a strong background of oral storytelling and the complexity and creativity in written narratives. Thus Chantee and Daniel are engaged in particular practices that are related to and are potentially supportive of literacy development. Their experience of listening to and singing rhymes and songs, as well as being immersed in oral storytelling, helps them to become familiar with different genres. It is also interesting to note that genre formats are not necessarily universal: for example what counts as a narrative or report in one culture may be quite different in another culture.

During lunch you have a few minutes to reflect on your morning observations. You are surprised at the amount of understanding the children have about literacy and how different their understandings seem to be. You think about ways of building a literacy picture of all the children, which would include reference to the literacy practices at home and wider community. As you begin to plan your afternoon observations, you think about what the term 'literacy' means: is it more than reading and writing? Michele, one of the carers, is interested in your notes and explains that the staff at the community family centre have been thinking about definitions of literacy. They are using the definition of literacy from the Australian Languages and Literacy Policy as the basis for their discussion. It states that literacy is:

> the ability to read and use information and to write appropriately in a range of contexts. It is used to develop knowledge and understanding, to achieve personal growth and to function effectively in our society. Literacy also includes the recognition of basic mathematical signs and symbols within texts. Literacy involves the integration of speaking, listening and critical thinking and reading and writing. Effective literacy is intrinsically purposeful, flexible and dynamic and continues to develop throughout an individual's lifetime.
>
> (Department of Employment, Education and Training 1991: 9)

On the basis of your lunchtime discussion with Michele you decide to spend the afternoon looking at different types of literacy practices and the ways the children's understandings about literacy are being supported and extended through particular activities. Michele identifies three major areas that are part of the toddlers' everyday literacy experiences at the centre. These are being developed to support literacy in ways that reflect some of the aspects identified in the above definition of literacy. Three areas are:

- environmental print
- story books
- the writing corner.

Using environmental print to support and extend literacy

Print in the environment

You decide to start with environmental print. It is clear from the moment that you entered the community family day care centre that the children are immersed in a print-rich environment. This consists of posters, charts and tables as well as interactive and ongoing information in a range of different languages. You notice that the feeding area has a hand-written poster with 'Name, formula, how given' across the top, alongside there is another poster with 'Name, meal time, sleep time, home time messages'. Just below the posters there are series of leaflets, in several languages, about different aspects of care, inviting parents and guardians to take one and add new ones. You are impressed by the amount of babies' and toddlers' work displayed and labelled, for example The Teddy Bears Picnic (by the babies!), marble paintings, 'Siapa nama anda?' (What is your name?) and 'Look at our Nien' (Chinese New Year monsters). Almost every available space is taken up by the children's work, hanging from the ceiling and covering the walls. There is a frieze, decorated by the toddlers with their birthdays written on, displayed at eye level. You also notice that there are several different scripts, including Khmer, Mandarin, Indonesian and German. You notice a list of handwritten words and phrases with English translations, such as 'Abba – dad, appa – sister, amma – mum' and 'Na, na – no, Afi Je – Here it is'. You wonder how the adults and children use the environmental print and eagerly start to take notes.

The room is alive with the sound of different languages. Parents are encouraged to stay, carers are employed on the basis of their cultural and linguistic background, and students on work experience and teaching practice are encouraged to use their linguistic repertoire. There is a deliberate attempt to match the children's linguistic and cultural background with their experiences at the centre. The carers have created a multilingual print-rich environment, by involving where possible the children's family members, student helpers and outside support organizations. As the day progresses, you notice a number of incidental references to the environmental print in the babies' and toddlers' room.

Incidental use of print in the environment

During the afternoon, the children are asked to find their names and birthdays as part of a game and a song. Where possible some of the children's names are written in their home language as well as English and the carer often refers to the two scripts. The carers point to notices about washing hands and ask the children to 'read' their favourite food at snack and lunch time. Children are comforted by being picked up and encouraged to look at the paintings, drawings and mobiles, while the carer reads the captions and names. You notice that some of the older children read the labels which they encounter every day, such as 'Please close the door', 'Toilet', 'The Teddy Bears Picnic' and 'Baby and toddler clinic' as they move from room to room. At snack time Annalise, who is 2 year and 6 months, places all the *A*s, from her alphabet spaghetti, around her edge of her dish. The carer comments on this by referring to the relationship between the sound and the symbol, 'Oh, look . . . *A* for Annalise, what does it say? *A* – Annalise.' Several children count the five 'currant buns' which they have painted and stuck on the window, accompanied by numbers *1* to *5*. During the afternoon the 'currant buns' are taken down and used as a visual aid for the song. As well as these incidental and spontaneous uses of environmental print, the carers also plan specific activities using the environmental print. There is much interaction in the home corner and around the Chinese New Year display.

Planned activities using environmental print

Structured play is seen as central to literacy learning. The structured play area is created to build on the children's experiences and has included a cafe and a clinic; today it is a kitchen. While playing in the kitchen, the carer involves two children in a number of literacy practices using environmental print. Among the note pads, telephone directory, greetings cards, reminder notes, advertisements from local pizza and Chinese takeaway restaurants, newspaper and TV guide, are a variety of recipe books. The carer locates the centre recipe books and invites Jenny (24 months) and Katia (18 months) to help her find pikelets (an Australian recipe) which they are going to make for Michael's birthday. After discussing birthday parties and reading the recipe, they make a shopping list. Jenny lists the ingredients and the carer writes them down. Meanwhile Katia has found a pile of catalogues and located the toy section, naming and claiming various toys. The carer then points to the cooking utensils, and talks about what they need to make pikelets.

Nearby, in the writing corner, children are invited to make a Chinese New Year card. A carer points to a Happy New Year banner written in Chinese and the Chinese New Year cards pinned to the wall, among a display of Chinese decorations. Jessica, 3 years 2 months, proudly announces that she has written her card in Chinese. This is disputed laughingly by Su Mei, almost 3 years, who comes from a Chinese background and recognizes some of the Chinese symbols. The carer praises Jessica and asks her what she has written, while encouraging Su Mei to write her own card. Su Mei points to each character and reads 'Kong hee fatt choy' (Happy New Year).

What are the children learning about literacy through their interaction with environmental print?

Here we see children learning about literacy through their use of the print around the centre. They are learning that print can be used to give and organize information, give instructions, denote ownership, send messages, depict a song, tell a story and recount an event. They are learning that print is meaningful and that it serves many different purposes; they are beginning to recognize the *functions* of print. Much of the environmental print in the family centre is contextualized, that is, its meaning can be derived from the surrounding context. For example, photographs of each child's family members, accompanied by a written caption and each person's name, helps them to make connections between the pictures and the writing. Researchers suggest that children begin to make meaning from print through the context in which the text occurs; that initially children 'read' environmental clues and not the actual print (Goodman 1983; Masonheimer *et al.* 1984; Goswami 1994).

The role of the adult is thought to be important in helping children make sense of environmental print. It is argued that children do not become readers and writers through mere exposure to environmental print. Laminack (1991: 88) argues that 'It is through meaningful interaction with others that young children begin to make connections between their own words, ideas and experiences and print.'

Thus through interaction with others, children become aware of the *forms* as well as the *functions of print*. Through activities that are personally and socially significant, children become curious about signs and symbols. For example, a strong desire to write a Chinese New Year card, find a name, send a message, or make sure that the shopping list includes all the ingredients to make pikelets, leads the child to experiment with letters, words, signs and symbols and make guesses about meaning. Su Mei is actually beginning to identify and comment on the differences between scripts. It is through observation, interaction, experimentation and talk about literacy in the environment that children begin to learn how to do literacy and what literacy entails. Laminack (1991) argues that there are a number of clues that children can use in order to construct meaning from environmental print. Miller (1996: 79) summarizes these under four headings:

- the general context – logos, the total packaging;
- graphics – size, colour, format, lettering;
- meaning – the object the print occurs on;
- other clues – specific to the individual child.

So environmental print does seem to have an important contribution to make to early reading and writing, but it is only one form of written language. Hall (1987: 28), summarizing research from a number of sources, argues that 'experience with environmental print is an intrinsic part of becoming a literate language user, but that such experiences operate in conjunction with many other oral and written language experiences'. In the context of the community family day centre the carers are using environmental print in a number of different ways to support the development of literacy. Not only are they drawing children's attention to the functions and forms of print, they are also encouraging children to use and create print for a number of different purposes. The carers recognize the importance of valuing family and community languages. They have created a multilingual environment in which the children are encouraged to experiment with print as part of their everyday experiences in the community family centre.

What will observations of other types of literacy activity reveal about the process of becoming literate? You go over to the book corner and sit on a cushion with Jamie, Anna and one of the carers, Cara.

Sharing story books to support and extend early literacy

The carer is in the book corner with Jamie (aged 9 months) and Anna (who is almost 3 years) sitting on her knee. Anna has picked up two books and asks the carer to read *Are You my Mother?* It soon becomes apparent that Anna knows the story as she joins in, pointing to the pictures and speaking with appropriate intonation. The following dialogue emerges:

Cara: Oh, your favourite! Shall we read it together, what does the little duck say? Are you my mother? . . . Are you my mother?

Anna: Are you my mother . . .

Cara: . . . I'm not your mother . . . I'm a dog.

Anna: I'm not your mother . . . I'm a dog (the carer turns the page and points to the words, as Anna points to the pictures. Anna seems to look from the picture to the words and back again, as she is telling the story).

Cara and Anna: Are you my mother? . . . I'm not your mother . . . I'm a hen.

Cara: What does the hen say? . . . Cluck, cluck, cluck, cluck (the carer smiles at Jamie and repeats cluck, cluck, cluck. Jamie squeals and bangs the page. The carer turns the page).

Anna and Cara: Are you my mother . . . I'm not your mother . . . I'm a pussy.

Cara: What does the pussy say?

Anna: Miaow, miaow, I'm not your mother (again the carer repeats the noises to Jamie and turns the page).

Anna and Cara: Are you my mother . . . I'm not your mother . . . I'm a dog.

Anna: What doggy say?

Cara: You know what a dog says, woof, woof, doesn't it, Jamie, woof woof.

Anna: Woof, woof.

 (The story continues in a similar vein. Later on the carer attempts to turn the page.)

Anna: No, let me, let me, me do.

Cara: You turn the page gently, turn it gently, this way, look, gently.

Anna: Gently.

 (At that moment Stuart, a student carer, walks past. He has been asked to collect evidence from two children about the concepts of print.)

Stuart: Oh what are you reading, Anna?

Anna: Are you my mother!

Stuart: Can you show me the front, where does it say that?

(Anna turns the book over and taps on the cover.)

Cara: What's it called?

 (Anna points to the front and back cover and runs her fingers over the words on both pages.)

Anna: Are you my mother? Are you my mother?

Cara: You are a clever girl.

Anna: Are you my mother? (Anna reads, pointing at the title words. At this point Anna notices that the spine is torn and cries out) Aw it's broked, broked oh look broked!

Cara: Oh yes, it's all right we can mend it, I'll mend it, later, I'll mend it later.

Anna: Mend it (Anna finds her place with the help of the carer, who points to the words and continues).
Cara: Here you are, start here . . . here . . . what does it say? Let's read it together . . . I'm not your mother, I'm a . . .
(Towards the end of the story Anna varies the pattern.)
Anna: I did have a mother, I did have a mother, I want to go home, I want my mother . . . (turns the page).
Anna: You're not a dog, you're not a cat, you're not a hen, you're not a pussy, you're my mother! Ah! (Anna ends on a note of glee, and then points to the words 'The end') The end!
Cara: That's right, the end. It had a happy ending, didn't it?
Anna: Happy ending, again, again, read again (turning to the front).

During this time Jamie snuggles up to Cara and seems to be focusing on the pictures, listening, enjoying the animal noises and occasionally touching the pages. For Jamie this literacy experience may suggest that storytelling is about positive relationships, having fun and doing something together. Cara occasionally asks Jamie about the pictures by describing and directing his attention to the illustrations, while responding to his babbling. In these early encounters with books Jamie is responding and interacting, Cara is initiating and leading.

Anna knows a great deal about storytelling, and wants to take the initiative and lead Cara through the book. The above transcript gives some insight into the way Anna is constructing and testing her view of a particular literacy practice: story reading. Her talk and actions suggests that she is beginning to make the following hypotheses about print:

• print is constant and carries a message;
• there is a relationship between the pictures and the words;
• print has a particular orientation;
• there is particular language to talk about print and reading;
• stories have particular structures;
• stories have particular types of language;
• stories have titles which are somewhere on the back or front cover;
• books are precious and should not be damaged;
• reading can be a shared and enjoyable experience.

What are the children learning about literacy through sharing the story?

Cara plays an important role in Anna's construction of meaning. Cara is engaged in what has been termed 'scaffolding' (Bruner 1977); she is providing Anna with support to enable her to share the story. This notion is based on Vygotsky's concept of the zone of proximal development, whereby what the child can do today in collaboration she can do tomorrow by herself. Snow and Nino (1986) argue that by providing a predictable and supportive framework, the adult enables the child to participate in the construction of meaning while learning about how reading is 'done' in a particular context. Several researchers have found that the nature of scaffolding changes and is reduced as the child becomes familiar with the book and matures (Snow and Nino 1986; Geekie and Raban 1993).

Scaffolding is evident from the way in which Cara invites Anna to read the story with her, treating her like a reader. She points to the words and reads, modelling the process, then goes back to the beginning of the sentence and starts again. Anna joins in immediately. Cara models the next sequence, and Anna eagerly repeats her words, pointing to the pictures. From then on Anna tells the story in unison with Cara. She knows about the sequence and is using the pictures as clues to each animal. Cara is also scaffolding by means of a question-and-answer sequence. Interestingly, Anna asks Cara the same question that she has been asked, about animal noises. It is as if she thinks that this is a game, part of the reading processes, in which you both know the answer, but you ask the question anyway. Cara is also teaching Anna about book handling skills as she talks to Anna about turning the pages.

It would seem that Anna's experiences and expectations about shared reading match Cara's. Thus this literacy event is potentially meaningful and enriching. It also gives Cara some insight into Anna's understanding of story reading. However, research suggests that the process and procedures that surround not only shared book encounters but all literacy events differ according to the cultural and social context in which they occur (Heath 1983). Anstey and Bull (1996: 158) argue that 'a critical feature emerging from the research is that there is no one set of literacy practices common to all communities . . . many different literacies are potentially available in each community'. Breen *et al.* (1994) and Anstey *et al.* (1994) found a diversity of literacy practices across families and communities, but a uniformity of literacy practices across schools. The implications of this apparent discrepancy between home and school literacy practices are far-reaching in terms of the potential achievement of children from a range of cultural and linguistic backgrounds. The effects of this mismatch may begin as soon as children enter formal care and education.

In addition to all the above, Anna is also learning about particular values and beliefs which are inherent in the story. She is learning about mother-child relationships and the importance of kinship: that someone else's mother cannot be a substitute for your own mother; that being without your mother or losing your mother is stressful and if you search long enough you may find her; that finding your mother is joyful and comforting. This is one particular view of a mother. The carers meet regularly to change and select new books. They have designed selection criteria to guide their choices; they discuss the way in which new books can be used with different children. Recognition of social, cultural and linguistic diversity within the centre and wider society is a number one priority.

Carers are conscious of the power of stories to convey values, attitudes and concepts and, with family members, are discussing ways of introducing *critical literacy* practices into the early years curriculum. Critical literacy involves analysing and challenging both overt and hidden messages within texts. The carers have begun by thinking about ways of using the following questions from Hill (1995: 24), as a means of exploring the relationships between language and power in text:

- Who are the texts representing?
- Whose experiences are made relevant?
- What is being learned and by who?

Playing in the writing corner as a means of supporting and extending literacy

You are keen to see what is happening in the writing corner. Just as you sit down nearby and begin to write, Noreen, who is 3, asks you what you are doing. You show her your notebook. After persuading you to give her a piece of paper and a pen, she sits next to you and starts to make marks on her paper, while looking around the room. She appears to be copying you. The writing corner is a new addition to the babies' and toddlers' room. The carers noticed that children engage in drawing and making marks as part of their art activities. Occasionally the older children bring in writing that has been done at home. The carers frequently refer to the print in the environment and use print materials as part of structured play. The carers decided that they would like to capitalize on the other areas in which the children appear to be engaged in literacy practices and the texts that children that bring from home, by adding a writing corner.

'Real' writing materials are placed on and around the table: writing paper, airmail paper, writing pads, memo pads, sticky pads, large sheets of butchers' paper, home-made recipe books, a book entitled *Can You Find Your Name?*, old diaries, address books, a calendar, an accounts book, greetings cards in different languages, pencils, pens and highlighters. Because of the nature of the materials, the carers agreed that an adult would oversee the table, to ensure that the younger children did not come to any harm. Some of the carers were concerned that the children's attempts at making marks should always be part of a meaningful context. They argued that children begin to make marks in order to communicate a message and that therefore literacy events should be embedded in a social context. So although some of the carers just wanted to 'see what the kids can do', it was agreed that initially a number of specific writing activities would be provided.

Annalise, 2 years and 6 months, is sitting at the writing table with her mum. She has brought her new alphabet book and is busily writing, talking eagerly while she does so. Annalise asks a question about the book. Her mum replies, 'He's doing the alphabet, this is the alphabet.' Anna repeats 'alphabet' several times and sings random letters as she draws. There is a constant dialogue about the book. Annalise also likes writing at home. Figures 3.1 to 3.3 (pages 67–9) show three examples of her writing during April and May. Her mum has written what Annalise actually said underneath.

May Ling, a carer, is writing a large Chinese New Year card to go in the entrance hall. Su Mei wanders over, and May Ling invites Jessica and Su Mei to make a Chinese New Year card, talking to them about what she is doing. She encourages Su Mei to write, she refuses, so May Ling writes the Chinese characters for her. Very carefully and with great concentration, Su Mei copies the carer's writing and then proudly reads it back, saying 'Kong hee fatt

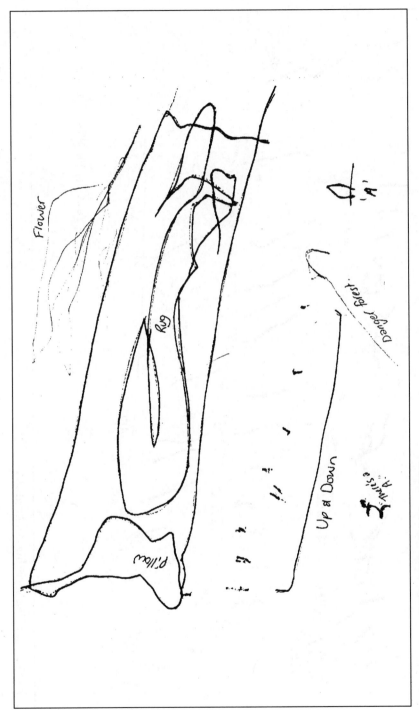

Figure 3.1 Annalise's writing (24 May 1996)

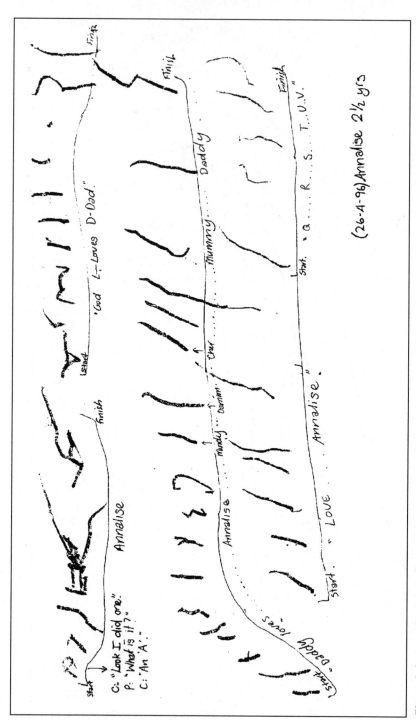

Figure 3.2 Annalise's writing (26 April 1996)

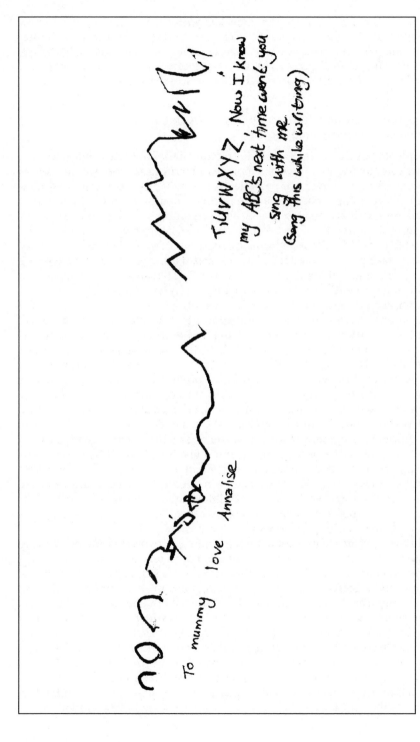

Figure 3.3 Annalise's writing (2 May 1996)

choy.' At the request of the carer, Su Mei writes her name in English, producing 'SuMi'. Jessica accepts the invitation to make a card without hesita-
tion. She seems to make marks which resemble Chinese and English script,
saying, 'This says "Happy New Year".' Su Mei insists that Jessica's writing is
not Chinese. Jessica also writes her name, in which the *J* is identifiable

What are the children learning about literacy through their involvement in the writing corner?

In order to build up a comprehensive picture of the children's understanding
of writing, many encounters with print and writing samples would have to
be considered. However, it is possible to identify some elements in these children's developing understanding of print. Annalise's mum explains that
Annalise has been making marks and scribbling since she was about 18
months old. Annalise is always included in social or religious events, many
of which involve different forms of literacy. Many of her early forms of
writing take place in joint activities, such as signing greeting cards, sending
invitations and making shopping lists. Annalise has also been encouraged to
write independently, which may explain the way she confidently engaged in
writing at the writing table with little prompting.

From the above samples, it would appear that Annalise has begun to recognize the difference between drawing and writing. In sample 1 she has
named the objects in her picture and identified an *A* which she has written in
two places. Harste *et al.* (1984) found that children in their study moved
freely between drawing and writing and often drew what they could not
write in order to convey what they wanted to communicate. The alphabet
seems to fascinate Annalise, and she has spent a great deal of time claiming
to write the alphabet. In samples 2 and 3 she has identified each letter as she
is writing, by singing. Interestingly, she begins by making separate marks
and then draws one continuous up and down line; both of these represent
the alphabet. *A* is beginning to emerge as an identifiable and recognizable
symbol; this is no accident as her first name begins with *A* and Annalise
claims she has written her name. Children are encouraged to write their
names on all their work. She also suggests that it is no longer necessary for
her mum to sing along, as now she knows her ABC.

Su Mei appears to have some understanding of two very different writing
systems. She recognizes some Chinese characters and can distinguish
between Chinese and English scripts. Her accuracy in copying the Chinese
characters suggests that she has had opportunities to practise Chinese
writing in other literacy contexts. Her desire to copy the Chinese characters
may stem from her experience in activities in which accuracy is seen as
important. Her comments to Jessica may suggest that she recognizes that
symbols have particular meanings and are represented in consistent ways.
On the other hand, she attempts to write her name in English and is comfortable with the result, even though she has omitted some letters. It would
seem that she is beginning to understand about print orientation in English
and possibly in Chinese. She assigns a message to her own symbols and is

aware that print carries a message; she clearly distinguishes between writing and drawing and can write her name in English using known letters.

Jessica is a few months older than Su Mei and is just beginning to make marks on the paper. Jessica differentiates between writing and drawing and seems happy to write independently. She appears to have used a combination of Chinese and English symbols from around the writing table. She has assigned a message to her writing and claimed that it is Chinese, although she has not distinguished between the scripts in her mark making. She did not appear to use any particular directionality except when writing her name. She pointed to the marks randomly when reading her writing to the carer and Su Mei, although she could identify her name by pointing to the letter *J*.

In all the above examples, the adult is sensitive to each child's needs and level of competence. The knowledge the children bring is valued and used. Their curiosity and attempts to make meaning are encouraged. The adults are modelling the process of writing for particular purposes. You experience this at first hand as Noreen asks you if you would like her 'notes' to go with your notes. The adults are demonstrating the connection between oral and written language and encouraging children to notice the difference between scripts. They demonstrate that writing communicates a message, is purposeful and is usually aimed at a particular audience. They also to a lesser extent focus on the way print works, pointing out print concepts and conventions, when appropriate.

The above discussion may suggest that the children are simply at different stages of writing development. Indeed, several researchers claim that early writing consists of a clear developmental sequence, characterized by progression through a series of identifiable and hierarchical stages (Ferreiro and Teberosky 1982; Goodman 1990). McNaughton (1995: 51) suggests that 'the physical and structural properties of the writing system and the motor and sensory systems needed for writing, together with the commonalities between children in their experience with cultural symbols may lead to some similarities'. However, he goes on to argue that fixed sequences do not account for the variation that occurs both by the same child over time and across children in sequences and stages. McNaughton comes to the conclusion that 'multiple sequences follow from learning and development systems within different literacy activities. Within this potential for diversity is the possibility of close similarity in developmental sequences' (p. 51). Our beliefs about how children learn to write are important because they influence the way in which children's progress in writing is facilitated, documented and evaluated.

Where to next? Conclusions and questions

At the end of the day, as you are waiting for parents/carers to collect their children, you begin to reflect on the day's observations. In order to try and make sense of some of your thoughts you begin to construct a number of conclusions about early literacy. You start by making the following list:

- Literacy skills, attitudes and knowledge begin to develop at a very early age and are continuous. The family and community play a significant role in the child's literacy learning. Some children may be learning in a language other than English, other children may have access to more than one language and script and are becoming bilingual and biliterate.
- The construction of literacy emerges from involvement in social and cultural events in which literacy practices are embedded. Thus children's understandings about the purposes and practices of literacy and what actually counts as literacy differ according to their experiences.
- Literacy activities are not neutral. Events in which literacy practices occur and texts are used both reflect and construct particular ideas and values. Some literacy practices may be valued more than others.
- Literacy is multidimensional and involves both social and cognitive processes. Children's construction of knowledge about literacy is created and mediated through social interaction in which they are active participants, so adults have an important part to play in helping children to become literate.
- Reading and writing are interrelated and develop alongside oral language. Children encounter literacy as part of social or cultural events which may involve speaking, listening, reading and writing. Each language process informs and supports the other.

Finally on the basis of your reflections you jot down a number of questions to discuss with your colleagues at your own family centre:

1 How can we find out what children know about literacy through their involvement in social and cultural events at home and within the community?
2 How can we build on and extend children's literacy practices which take account of linguistic and cultural diversity in our centre and in the wider community? Can we incorporate the concept of 'multiple literacies' rather than just 'literacy' into our planning and evaluation?
3 How can we draw on the expertise and knowledge of each family to inform our language and literacy policy and practice, and try to ensure a match between home and centre literacy practices? Equally, how can we ensure that families have access to the ways in which we are meeting the aims of the centre?
4 How can we create and utilize a literacy environment which will give children the optimum opportunity to observe, participate and experiment with literacy in ways which are authentic and relevant?
5 Given the diversity of literacy practices, what is the role of the adults in our centre? How can we scaffold and extend children's literacy learning? How can we support those children with whom we do not share a first language?
6 How can sharing stories, rhymes and songs be used as a means of supporting and extending literacy?
7 What opportunities can we give our children to use forms of computerized technology such as CD-ROMs? How can we support the children's learning with these?

8 Finally, do we need to re-access our resources? Is it possible and desirable to find ways of helping children to begin to recognize the values and messages embedded within texts? How can we become critical literacy users?

References

Anstey, M. and Bull, G. (1996) *The Literacy Labyrinth*. Sydney: Prentice Hall.

Anstey, M., Bull, G., Freebody, P. and Luke, A. (1994) *Adult Literacy Practices in Rural Families and Communities*. Melbourne: NLLIA Monograph.

Breen, M., Louden, W., Barratt-Pugh, C., Rivalland, J., Rohl, M. and Rhydwen, M. (1994) *Literacy in its Place. Literacy Practices in Urban and Rural Communities*, Vol. 1. Canberra: Department of Employment, Education and Training.

Bruner, J. (1977) Early social interaction and language acquisition, in H. R. Schaffer (ed.) *Studies in Mother-Infant Interaction*. London: Academic Press.

Crawford, P. (1995) Early literacy: emerging perspectives, *Journal of Research in Childhood Education*, 10(1): 71–86.

Davis, L. (1995) *P. B. Bear's Birthday Party*. New York: Dorling Kindersley Multimedia.

Department of Employment, Education and Training (1991) *Australia's Language. The Australian Language and Literacy Policy*. Canberra: Australian Government Publishing Service.

Ferreiro, E. and Teberosky, A. (1982) *Literacy before Schooling*. Exeter, NH: Heinemann.

Geekie, P. and Raban, B. (1993) *Learning to Read and Write through Classroom Talk*. Stoke-on-Trent: Trentham Books.

Goodman, Y. (1983) Beginning reading development: strategies and principles, in R. Parker and F. Davis (eds) *Developing Literacy: Young Children's Use of Language*. Newark, DE: International Reading Association.

Goodman, Y. (1990) *How Children Construct Literacy*. Newark, DE: International Reading Association.

Goswami, U. (1994) Phonological skills, analogies and reading development, *Reading*, 28(2): 32–7.

Hall, N. (1987) *The Emergence of Literacy*. London: Hodder and Stoughton.

Harste, J., Woodward, V. and Burke, C. (1984) *Language Stories and Literacy Lessons*. Portsmouth, NH: Heinemann Educational.

Heath, S. B. (1983) *Ways with Words: Language, Life and Work in Communities and Classrooms*. Cambridge: Cambridge University Press.

Hiebert, E. H. (1978) Pre-school children's understanding of written language, *Child Development*, 49: 1231–4.

Hill, S. (1995) Early literacy and diversity, *Australian Journal of Early Childhood*, 20(1): 23–7.

Hudelson, S. (1994) Literacy development of second language children, in F. Genesee (ed.) *Educating Second Language Children: The Whole Child, the Whole Curriculum, the Whole Community*. Cambridge: Cambridge University Press.

Laminack, L. L. (1991) *Learning with Zachary*. Richmond Hill, Ontario: Ashton Scholastic.

Lofts, P. (1983) *How the Birds Got their Colours*. Sydney: Ashton Scholastic.

Luke, A. (1994) *The Social Construction of Literacy in the Classroom*. Melbourne: Macmillan.

Masonheimer, P. E., Drum, P. A. and Ellis, L. C. (1984) Does environmental print identification lead children into word reading? *Journal of Reading Behaviour*, 16: 257–71.

McNaughton, S. (1995) *Patterns of Emergent Literacy. Processes of Development and Transition*. Oxford: Oxford University Press.

Miller, L. (1996) *Towards Reading*. Buckingham: Open University Press.

Newkirk, T. (1989) *More than Stories: The Range of Children's Writing*. Portsmouth, NH: Heinemann.

Snow, C. and Nino, A. (1986) The contracts of literacy: what children learn from learning to read books, in W. Teale and E. Sulzby (eds) *Emergent Literacy: Writing and Reading*. Norwood, NJ: Ablex.

Snow, C., Barnes, W., Chandler, J., Goodman, I. and Hemphill, L. (1991) *Unfulfilled Expectations: Home and School Influences on Literacy*. Cambridge, MA: Harvard University Press.

Solsken, J. W. (1993) *Literacy, Gender, and Work in Families and in School*. Norwood, NJ: Ablex.

Strickland, D. and Morrow, L. (eds) (1989) *Emerging Literacy: Young Children Learn to Read and Write*. Newark, DE: International Reading Association.

Taylor, D. (1983) *Family Literacy: Young Children Learn to Read and Write*. Exeter, NH: Heinemann Educational.

Teale, W. H. and Sulzby, E. (eds) (1986) *Emergent Literacy: Writing and Reading*. Norwood, NJ: Ablex.

4 | 'Why d'you speak funny?' – supporting all children learning to talk and talking to learn

Caroline Barratt-Pugh

Introduction

One of my earliest childhood memories is what happened at my first day at a new school. We had moved from the south to the north of England. I was keen and eager in my new school uniform, ready to impress. During the first session I began to settle in and felt fairly comfortable with my new class. But, by the end of playtime I had resolved never to speak again and to go home as soon as possible, as several children crowded round me and asked, 'Why d'you speak funny?' Years later, as a teacher I renewed my interest in the power of language! I have worked with children and students during the past 20 years to develop my understanding of how language is learned and how we can best support that process. My teaching and research at Edith Cowan University has given me the opportunity to explore how the social and cultural contexts determine not only how children learn to talk but also what they can do with talk.

In this chapter I would like you to join the staff and parent/carers of a family community day care centre. They have decided to have a series of meetings to explore how children learn to talk, and talk to learn. Many of the children come from families where English is not the main or sole language. The staff are beginning by observing what the 0- to 3-year-olds do with language.

Meeting 1 – What can toddlers do with language?

All the staff agree to observe the language interactions of the youngest children in a number of different situations. They note down what the child does to get his or her message across and why the child is communicating. At the first staff meeting they unravel their observations and after sharing their findings they decide to construct three observation charts (Figures 4.1, 4.2 and 4.3).

The babies seem to:

- move from babbling and cooing to producing a range of sounds that have particular meanings;
- produce sounds that often reflect their home language, they appear to be tuning-in to sounds and intonation patterns;
- use gestures, facial expressions and pointing to indicate meaning;
- respond and interact with others in a way that reflects their cultural communicative style;
- show signs of understanding some words and simple commands, often in context.

Why are they communicating? They seem to:

- show distress, anxiety and demand attention;
- request objects or actions;
- show interest in others and respond to others;
- use greetings and farewells;
- draw attention to things in the immediate environment, people, events, objects.

Figure 4.1 Language development between 0 and 12 months

The babies seem to:

- move from one-word utterances (holophrases) to two/three-word utterances (telegraphic speech);
- convey complex meanings in one- and two-word utterances;
- use the same words to convey different meaning in different contexts;
- use one word to represent a whole category of animals, people, places and events;
- understand a great deal more than they can produce. That is, they seem to have more receptive than expressive language;
- use single words or simple phrases in more than one language, if they are growing up in a bilingual or multilingual context, or if English is their second language.

Why are they communicating? They seem to:

- build on and refine the language they have developed from birth;
- convey an increasing number of meanings using single words and short phrases, often based on here and now;
- draw attention to things in the immediate environment;
- make requests on the basis of immediate needs and wants;
- make observations about their immediate world;
- initiate contact and establish joint interaction;
- join-in simple routine games, songs, rhymes;
- move from labelling to describing and use language that reflects the important aspects of their daily lives.

Figure 4.2 Language development between 12 and 24 months

The toddlers seem to:

- combine two-word sentences, sentence length continues to increase;
- add to and extend sentences as vocabulary rapidly expands;
- use 'wh' question words and use rising intonation to ask questions;
- use more grammatically conventional sentences;
- overgeneralize general rules (wented, buyed), still learning about exceptions;
- use socially appropriate forms in relation to sociocultural norms;
- understand a range of different concepts.

Toddlers who are learning two languages simultaneously and becoming bilingual seem to:

- differentiate between two language systems;
- transfer rules and words from one language to the other;
- use appropriate language in relation to the context and speaker.

Why are they communicating? They seem to:

- use language to express most of their communicative needs;
- use language to convey a range of meanings;
- use language to move from here and now to past and future events;
- begin to retell stories which can be difficult to follow as sequencing and detail may be limited;
- express feelings and use imaginative language, particularly in dramatic play;
- have extended conversations;
- continue to develop their receptive language. This may include following more complex directions and instructions, understanding simple stories and understanding a range of different concepts.

Figure 4.3 Language development between 24 months and 3 years

At the end of the discussion the staff agree that this is useful information which they can use as a way of guiding their observations and mapping children's progress. They know that this should only be used as a general and flexible guide, as children's language development is not necessarily sequential or linear. Although research suggests that these attainments have been documented in babies all over the world, each child's acquisition of language is unique. Research suggests that patterns of development vary according to the interactive styles and child rearing practices within individual families.

Caregiver interactions with young children and the expectations and use of language vary according to the cultural and social background of the family (Heath 1983; Clancy 1986; Minami 1994). These differences are reflected not only in the way language is used but also in differences in vocabulary, grammar and pronunciation, referred to as dialects. Non-verbal communication is also culturally bound. Gestures, facial expressions, eye contact, body contact and use of personal space have different meanings in different cultures. Thus children learn about non-verbal communication, what language can be used for and conversational conditions and constraints through the sociocultural contexts in which they are growing up.

On the basis of this discussion Sally points out that there are differences within as well as across cultures. She suggests that they should add culturally specific information about interaction patterns to the chart as they continue to observe and discuss these with individual families. In order to avoid stereotypical assumptions about particular cultural backgrounds this information should come from the children's families. Sally starts by writing a note about the importance of not touching Wonapon or Aravan on the head, as their mum has explained that in their Thai family this is not acceptable. The group agree that it is important to value differences in cultural norms and dialects while helping children to use language appropriately in different contexts. The question remains as to who decides what is appropriate when and where.

Towards the end of the meeting Franca comments that they have begun to think about what children do in order to communicate and why they communicate. Now they need to find out more about how children learn to communicate in interactions with adults.

Meeting 2 – Adults and toddlers talking together

After discussing the advantages and disadvantages of different methods of recording, the staff and parents share their findings. They decide to place their interactions under the four types of talk identified in parental interactions with their children by Maclure (1992): shaping, sharing, supporting, stretching. As they explore each type of talk they try to identify the key features of each one.

The staff and parents/carers share their observations of very young children and discuss Madjid in particular. In each example the parents/carers respond to the children's utterances as if they are meaningful, they respond with verbal and physical gestures. They are relating actions to words and helping the baby to produce and respond to sounds. From the very first interactions, the baby is being initiated into the 'rules' of turn taking, which shapes their understanding of how conversation is 'done' (see Figure 4.4).

Madjid is 3 months old, lying in his cot, making cooing noises. I go over and start to talk, looking directly at him, gently tickling his tummy. 'Hello, have you woken up, have you?' Madjid begins to screech with delight and move his arms and legs. 'Oh yes, you like that?' Madjid squeals with delight again. 'Tickle your tummy, tickle your tummy.' I wait for a response then say 'again, again?' This continues for a few moments. I am smiling and I seem to be speaking in a high pitched voice.

Figure 4.4 Shaping talk

Michael, who is 26 months old, is talking to his mum as they get ready to leave the centre and go shopping.

Mum: Come on, let's go buy nana a present.
Michael: Nenunt?
Mum: Yeah, its nana's birthday.
Michael: Yeah, birfday
Mum: What shall we get, for nana?
Michael: Cake!
Mum: No, Auntie Bea gonna get a cake.
Michael: Antie Bea?
Mum: Yeah, You can choose a card . . . scarf, d'you think she'd like a scarf?
Michael: Scarf? Me scarf.
Mum: (laughs) No, its nana's birthday, we're gonna buy for nana. You get the card.
Michael: Card.

Figure 4.5 Sharing talk

As the staff and parent/carers discuss an interaction between Michael and his mum (Figure 4.5), they identify a number of similar examples of sharing talk. By sharing ideas, feelings and perspectives the child and the adult are developing intersubjectivity. That is, they are jointly constructing understandings about how the world works. For example, in Figure 4.5, Michael is learning about a cultural event that consists of particular rituals. In this case, the event involves buying and giving presents and cards, sharing a cake, choosing something nana will like and meeting different people. Even though they are discussing an abstract event Michael can join in because he has had previous experience of birthdays. Michael is involved in the process, his mum explains what they are going to do and asks Michael for ideas and opinions. He is given responsibility for choosing the card. His responses are treated seriously as his mum explains why he cannot have a scarf. Thus Michael is learning about a particular view of the world and his place in it. He uses repetition, which his mum extends. She interprets his single utterances as questions and responds to his comments with further explanation.

The example of supporting talk in Figure 4.6 is familiar to many of the staff and parents/carers. Research exploring the interaction between caregivers and young children has found that in many societies parents/caregivers seem to adapt their speech to young children (see Julia Gillen's discussion on CDS (child-directed speech) in the next chapter). Carers are able to give just the right amount of support to sustain the conversation while enabling the child to build up their linguistic repertoire. Bruner (1977) argued that this type of speech provides scaffolding, that is, a support system which enables the child to move in their zone of proximal development (Vygotsky 1978). He found that scaffolding started at birth and often occurred in highly predictable routines, such as bathing, eating, changing, dressing as well as in shared activities around an object or event and during play.

Martène is almost 2, she speaks French and English at home and is playing with some soft toys in the book corner. Marsha understands a little French.

Marsha: Bonjour Martène, what have you got?
Martène: (Martène holds the koala bear up to Marsha)
Marsha: A cuddly koala bear . . . ah, are you giving him a hug? (Marsha demonstrates with a toy rabbit)
Martène: Hug, hug.
Marsha: Ah, give him a big hug . . . oh that's nice, all soft and cuddly (Marsha strokes the rabbit).
Martène: Huh! (Martène throws the koala on the floor and laughs)
Marsha: Ah, pauvre koala, poor koala, pick him up . . .
Martène: Ah, pauvre Ko Ko . . .
Marsha: Oh, pick him up, give him a cuddle . . .
Martène: Oh, poor Ko Ko.
Marsha: That's better, give him a kiss and a cuddle.
Martène: Cuggle.
Marsha: Ah, that's right, give koala a cuddle.

Figure 4.6 Supporting talk

There are elements of supporting talk in Figures 4.4 and 4.5, but a number of additional aspects can be identified in Figure 4.6. Marsha responds to Martène's initial gesture by labelling the soft toy and then asking a question, while demonstrating what she means through her own actions. Martène imitates Marsha's action and repeats the key word. Marsha then confirms Martène's response by incorporating the single word into a complete utterance and expanding this by introducing a new concept which she demonstrates by stroking the koala. What happens next is very interesting, Martène seems to switch quite easily and naturally between English and French. Marsha uses the French word 'pauvre', thereby acknowledging and supporting Martène's attempt to use English and French. Marsha expands Martène's final utterance and models the correct pronunciation as part of the continuing conversation.

Zita explains that in the brief sequence given in Figure 4.7 she is extending the children's talk in a number of different ways. She provides new vocabulary as she labels the tea strainer and demonstrates what she means by pointing to it. She confirms and expands Susan's comment about her grandmother, following this with an open-ended question. She describes what she is doing and then explains what has happened. She helps both children to try this difficult task and changes her open-ended question to a closed one in order to help them respond, 'Where are they, where are the tea leaves . . . look.' Finally she builds on Anna's imagination by asking her to pretend to drink the tea. Anna seems to understand and repeats "tend'. Zita has also used a range of language functions, including explaining, talking about feelings, pretending and informing.

Anna is almost 3 years old; Susan is 18 months. They are playing in the home corner kitchen. The resources include a variety of utensils and cooking implements from the children's families, including a Japanese water spoon, an African calabash, a Chinese soup spoon, a wok, a colander and a variety of strainers. Zita has brought the teapot with cold tea left from lunch.

Zita: Can I have the tea strainer? (points to the tea strainer). Susan, can I have the tea strainer? That's it, yep, that's called a tea strainer.
Susan: Omar, Omar [German for grandma].
Zita: Has your Omar got a tea strainer? I wonder what she uses it for?
Susan: Tea!
Anna: Tea!
Zita: Yes, for tea! Does she pour the tea into the cup, look, look like this (demonstrates). Look . . . I'm pouring the tea.
Susan: Dis? (copies Zita)
Zita: Yep, it catches all the tea leaves, look, see, see all the tea leaves . . . in the tea strainer?
Anna: Leaves, me look, me!
Zita: You wanna go? Here pour the tea . . . look like this, hold the tea strainer and pour the . . . carefully so not to spill . . .
Anna: (pours the tea).
Zita: Oh what's happened to the tea leaves? . . . Where are they, where are the tea leaves . . . look.
Anna: (points)
Zita: There they are, look, the tea leaves, Susan's turn (Anna begins to drink the tea).
Zita: Oh, Anna, no it's not nice, it's cold, look just pretend, look like this (makes slurping noises). Just pretend . . . oh, I like tea, nice.
Anna: 'tend, nice (makes slurping noises).

Figure 4.7 Stretching talk

The group conclude that open-ended questions are a powerful means of expanding children's language and learning. They do not have correct answers; they encourage different responses; they encourage children to think about what they have done and describe it; they serve as a means of solving problems; they can encourage children to use more precise and specific vocabulary. They decided to create a list of open-ended questions and statements to help extend language and learning in relation to the functions they have identified.

The parents/carers agree that the four aspects of interaction – shaping, sharing, supporting and stretching – are not necessarily related to age or mutually exclusive. All four aspects may occur in one conversation and often they overlap. They also recognize that not all parents/carers use these particular strategies. Individual characteristics of the adult and child as well as the cultural context influence the type of interaction strategies preferred.

However, Michael suggests that these four aspects could be useful for helping them incorporate language into their planning and records.

The group agree that it is clear from the examples that have been discussed that their children, like all others, start to learn language from birth. All these examples demonstrate how children learn to convey meaning through mastery of these four aspects of interaction. However, Petra notes that in all the examples the driving force is the need to convey meaning. She suggests, therefore, that language is acquired through the desire to communicate, which is fostered through interaction with adults and other children. She uses the following quote to illustrate her own beliefs: 'Language . . . is a social process which is used to communicate what we know, feel and think. Through interaction with others, children not only explore their own thinking but modify and extend their ideas beyond their own personal experiences' (Neuman and Roskos 1993: 42).

Jasminder agrees, but asks if the process of learning to talk and talking to learn through interaction is the same for children who are bilingual or learning English as a second language.

Meeting 3 – Learning in two languages

Following on from Jasminder's question, Meeting 3 is used to explore issues about children who are becoming bilingual. The staff and parents/carers split into two groups. One member of each group has brought a case study for discussion and recommendations.

After a lengthy debate the group summarize their discussion and recommendations ready to report back to the rest of the parents/carers and staff.

There are many different ways of becoming bilingual, from simultaneous bilingualism (where two or more languages are learned together from birth), to successive bilingualism (where one language is learned after the first one has been acquired). There are many variations within these two types of development. Romaine (1991) has identified six types of bilingual acquisition, which vary according to the broad social context, the immediate community, family members and individual preferences. In the case given in Figure 4.8, Catherine appears to be learning two languages successively.

Catherine is new to the centre. Catherine's mum is very concerned about Catherine's language development. All the family speak Cantonese at home and she is worried that this will interfere with her development of English. Mum wants her to learn English as she needs this to succeed at school and have access to wider society. Her older sister, Claire, maintains that she doesn't speak Cantonese and talks to Catherine in English. I am responsible for monitoring Catherine's progress at the centre and I am worried that she is reluctant to speak in either language and appears to be withdrawn. What shall I do?

Figure 4.8 Group 1's case study – presented by Narghis

Research suggests that learning in two languages is very positive in relation to:

- Social and cultural development. Catherine is learning about her Chinese heritage, customs and norms through her everyday interactions in Cantonese. Cantonese enables her to communicate with her family and the Chinese community. She needs Cantonese in order to speak to her grandparents. For some children their home language is the only language that is spoken at home, thus maintenance is essential for communication with primary carers.
- Emotional development. Language embodies our sense of who we are and how we feel about ourselves, our families and our world. Thus in order to promote positive self-esteem and emotional well-being Catherine needs to be able to use Cantonese in the centre and feel that her language and therefore her self is a valued and integral part of the centre.
- Cognitive development. There have been several studies which suggest that fluent bilingualism actually promotes divergent and creative thinking, metalinguistic awareness and communicative sensitivity. Thus learning Cantonese and English could potentially enhance Catherine's cognitive development (Cummins 1976).

They conclude that bilingualism is a very positive and desirable attribute!

However, it is important to recognize and take into account the parents' concern, by talking to them and finding out what they think is best. Bilingual carers can discuss the way in which two languages develop and support each other, stressing the importance of using their language(s) at home. Jasminder remembers being told not to use Punjabi when she went to school and Veasna admits that he can no longer speak Khmer, which is his first language. Catherine's reluctance to use Cantonese may be related to the attitude of her older sister, who seems to be rejecting her first language. The centre needs to show Catherine and her parents that their home language is valued and to encourage her to use Cantonese while she begins to feel comfortable using English. It is important to continue to support the development of both languages, but perhaps keep them separate if possible. The group list a number of recommendations:

- talk to mum; if she agrees, continue to use Cantonese to help Catherine settle in;
- encourage play with other Cantonese-speaking children;
- demonstrate the value of Cantonese in as many ways as possible: tapes, stories, songs, music, print;
- ensure that the choice of activities and materials represents Catherine's cultural background;
- observe Catherine in different situations, to ascertain if she is ready to begin using English;
- do not put pressure on her to use English: maybe she is just getting used to the centre – there is often a silent period when children tune-in to a new language;

- give her the opportunity to listen to songs, nursery rhymes and stories that have predictable and repetitive story lines, so she can join in when she's ready;
- use visual aids and gestures to help relate actions to words.

The second group have been discussing Kristov who speaks Polish and some English (Figure 4.9).

Group 2 summarize their discussion for the rest of the group. They conclude that what is happening is very positive. What Jasminder has observed is a demonstration of rapid development. Kristov shows some sophisticated understanding about language. Already he appears to differentiate between contexts: Polish at home with parents and siblings, English in the centre with peers and carers. He has found a strategy for getting information about English ('say this') and appears to be reasonably comfortable using English. His use of phrases has been identified as formulaic speech; it may be helping Kristov to join in activities, get into conversations and get feedback on which to build his fluency. His code switching may occur for a variety of reasons, but it is a positive strategy rather than something to worry about. Kristov has two language resources to draw on, so the parents/carers need to work out from the other words and the context what he means, so that he doesn't get frustrated. The grammatical errors seem to be similar to those made by first language speakers and could be part of the developmental process. However, staff need to be aware of possible transfer from his first language just so they can note this on his profile and mention it to his next carer. Here are their recommendations.

- encourage him to use the language he feels most comfortable with;
- continue to value and use Polish where possible;
- ensure language is part of the activity and that the activity is appropriate for his cognitive level;
- use visual aids and concrete activities to support meaning;
- be aware of our own use of English, speak 'naturally', don't use exaggerated intonation or shout;
- use non-verbal communication to help get meaning across, but be aware of different cultural conventions of gestures and body language;

Kristov has been at the centre for six months. He speaks Polish at home. As he has grown in confidence he tends to use English at the centre and has made English-speaking friends. I am concerned because he seems to switch between languages, make a number of grammatical mistakes and get frustrated when he can't express what he wants to say. He's very sociable and joins other children, often using phrases that don't always make sense. He often says 'say this' accompanied by gestures, which means 'tell me what it is, or does'. How can I help? Should I correct his English? What should I be doing to help increase his fluency in English? Will this interfere with his Polish?

Figure 4.9 Group 2's case study – presented by Jasminder

- use whole phrases and try to be consistent initially;
- involve the child in activities that give access to patterns of language and repetition, such as games;
- focus on the meaning of the message rather than the way in which the message is being conveyed;
- respond positively to errors by modelling target utterance as part of the conversation;
- find out about differences between English and Polish to help become aware of potential difficulties.

The group concluded that in this context, the process of second language development may be very similar to first language development, but parents/carers need to be more aware of the language they use and the contexts that best support Kristov's language and learning.

After sharing their case studies, Jasminder adds that the importance of supporting children's home languages from an early age has been well documented (Cummins 1976; Skutnabb-Kangas 1981; Breen *et al.* 1994; Makin *et al.* 1995). Although there is much debate about the 'best way' to support bilingual development, the reality is that children are growing up in a range of bilingual contexts. Thus ways of supporting development can best be established, through knowledge of the bilingual context and consultation with the families and communities involved. This may entail a shift in the relationship between the centre and the family/community as notions of expertise and power are renegotiated. Clearly understanding the children's linguistic and cultural background is very important to ensure that provision and practice is appropriate at the centre. This understanding begins by building a partnership with each family.

Meeting 4 – Communication between families and the centre

Kelly (a member of staff) and Angela (a parent) present some of their considered views. Angela, Annalise's mum, says that the partnership between families and the centre is a two-way process. She likes to know what's happening in the centre and shows the group a book she uses to record what Annalise does at the centre. Each day a carer fills the book in and Angela completes it on the basis of Annalise's comments at the end of the day. On occasions Annalise decides she has had enough of being questioned and asks Angela about *her* day recording Angela's response in the journal.

Kelly explains that getting to know each family takes place over a long period of time as a relationship of trust and understanding is established. She argues that mutual trust and support are not easy when there are differences between religious beliefs, gender roles, dress and food codes, family expectations and child rearing practices. She believes that discussions, therefore, should be a two-way process in which an exchange of information takes place in a sensitive and confidential way. Kelly suggests that both the centre staff and the parents/carers record what they feel is important to know about.

Centre staff: we would like to know about
- language, culture and religion;
- attitude toward use of home language;
- special needs;
- child rearing and health practices;
- the family's expectations of the centre;
- the child's interests, likes, dislikes;
- any other aspects that the parents/carers feel are important, particularly in relation to circumstances that may be causing anxiety or stress.

Parents/carers: we would like to know about
- expectations about our kids;
- how the centre works – times, routines, meal times;
- carers – languages, roles, responsibilities;
- policies on different aspects of development – health, etc.;
- services and other professionals available;
- what your goals are and how you plan;
- our involvement and contribution.

Kelly argues that as they build up a picture of families and community which is constantly changing, they should try to ensure that the environment represents the diversity of families. Already children are given opportunities to hear, see and use different languages, including Braille and sign language. Information around the centre is written in several languages and changed or added to as new children arrive. Information from and for parents/carers is written in different languages and interpreters are available to support communication between the family and centre. Makin *et al.* (1995: 83) argue that 'Ideally, each child should find reflected in the people, the languages and the play materials, elements that are familiar and elements that are new so that the centre mirrors the diverse nature of the wider world.' In the next meeting they decide to look at how the activities in the centre reflect and support language and learning.

Meeting 5 – Creating a context for learning to talk and talking to learn

The group have made notes on three particular aspects of the centre which they feel are central in helping children to learn to talk and talk to learn. They are play, songs/rhymes and stories. They discuss the various ways in which they can extend their use of these to encourage learning. During this process they cover many of the aspects of language learning described by myself in Chapter 3 and by Julia Gillen in Chapter 5.

Meeting 6 – Planning for interaction

On the basis of their previous observations and discussion the group decide to spend the next meeting looking at ways of planning to support different types of interaction, which recognize both language and gender differences. As well as helping children to become independent through making decisions about where, with whom and what they play, it is also important to offer a range of opportunities for children to experience a variety of group interactions. The group find that they cannot agree about all aspects of organization, but decide to list possible groupings and try them out over a period of time, observing carefully what the effect of these changes is on the way children interact.

Group organization could be based on:

- same-language groups;
- mixed-language groups;
- access to adults as well as children who speak different languages;
- individual, pair and collaborative activities;
- single-gender groups, especially in areas where one gender seems to dominate;
- positive role models.

Jasminder says that it is important to consider *what* we say to children as well as *how* we actually get them to talk. She explains that it is not only songs, rhymes and books that present a particular view of the world, but the very language we use. That is, language not only conveys meaning but it also constructs meaning. She argues that the words we choose and the way we put them together actually construct the meaning we convey to the children. She uses an example to illustrate her claim. The following three statements have all been used to describe François and Martène who speak English and French. 'They're becoming bilingual'; 'They come from a non-English-speaking background'; 'They don't have any language yet.' Jasminder claims that each statement reflects a particular view of François and Martène and an attitude to learning more than one language. Jasminder argues that it is important to be aware of the language we use and how it presents a particular view of the world which influences the developing attitudes and values of even the very young children. Nerrida thinks about all the times she has said 'can I have two big strong boys', and Zita thinks how strange and difficult it seems to use 'postperson' or 'workpeople'. The task of monitoring their language seems huge. Jasminder suggests they look at *Genderwatch* (Myers 1987), a book of self-assessment schedules for use in care and education contexts, as a starting point.

Meeting 7 – Developing a language policy

The group decide to use all the information they have collected, shared and analysed to begin to write a language policy. They start by asking the following questions:

1 Learning to use language
- What are our views on the way in which language is learned?
- How do these views influence our provision and practice?

2 Relationship between families and the centre
- How do we communicate with our families?
- Are we building a genuine partnership and consultation process?
- What opportunities do family members have to talk to us and be involved in the centre?
- Is information freely available and provided in the languages of our families?

3 Supporting bidialectal/bilingual and multilingual children
- How can we find out about the languages spoken at home?
- How can we support children's home languages and dialects?
- How can we help to foster the development of English alongside home languages?
- What role does the family and community play in planning and supporting the needs of children who are becoming bilingual?

4 Interaction
- Do we interact with children for many different purposes? What do we use language for most of the time?
- How do we interact with children at different levels of development?
- What strategies do we use to extend children's talk?
- How do we help children to initiate and take the lead in conversations?
- How do we deal with sexist and racist comments?

5 Activities
- Do the activities and resources reflect the diversity of our families and wider community?
- Do the activities enable children to use different levels of language and understanding?
- Do the activities provide opportunities for the children to use language for different purposes?
- How can we use dramatic play and stories to help children move from here and now to more abstract language?

6 Planning and monitoring talk
- How can we incorporate language into our planning?
- How do we monitor and record the children's use of language(s)?
- How can we monitor our own talk, particularly in relation to gender-inclusive language?
- How can we involve parents/carers in jointly describing the children's language development?

Nadia suggests that the policy on language should also include reference to literacy, as these two aspects of learning are interrelated. The parents/carers and the centre staff agree. Nadia has been invited to spend the day at a nearby community family day care centre looking specifically at the way children learn about literacy. The group eagerly await her report before they write their policy on language and literacy.

Finally I would like to thank the childcare workers, parents and children in the Family Day Care Centres for their insights and enthusiasm during our discussions which led to these two chapters.

References

Breen, M., Louden, W., Barratt-Pugh, C., Rivalland, J., Rohl, M. and Rhydwen, M. (1994) *Literacy in its Place. Literacy Practices in Urban and Rural Communities*, Vol. 1. Canberra: DEET.

Bruner, J. (1977) Early social interaction and language acquisition, in H. R. Schaffer (ed.) *Studies in Mother–Infant Interaction*. London: Academic Press.

Clancy, P. M. (1986) The acquisition of communicative style in Japanese, in B. Schieffelin and E. Ochs (eds) *Language Socialization across Cultures*. Cambridge: Cambridge University Press.

Cummins, J. (1976) The influence of bilingualism on cognitive growth: a synthesis of research findings and explanatory hypotheses, *Working Papers on Bilingualism*, 9: 1–43.

Heath, S. B. (1983) *Ways with Words. Life and Work in Classrooms and Communities*. Cambridge: Cambridge University Press.

Maclure, M. (1992) The first five years, in K. Norman (ed.) *Thinking Voices: The Work of the National Oracy Project*. London: Hodder and Stoughton.

Makin, L., Campbell, J. and Diaz, C. (1995) *One Childhood, Many Languages*. Pymbye, NSW: Harper Educational.

Minami, M. (1994) Long conversational turns or frequent turn exchanges: cross-cultural comparison of parental narrative elicitation, paper presented at the Annual Boston University Conference on Language Development. (18th Boston, MA.) ED 368202.

Myers, K. (1987) *Genderwatch. Self-assessment Schedules for Use in Schools*. London: Schools Curriculum Development Council.

Neuman, S. and Roskos, K. (1993) *Language and Literacy Learning in the Early Years. An Integrated Approach*. London: Harcourt Brace.

Romaine, S. (1991) *Languages in Australia*. Cambridge: Cambridge University Press.

Skutnabb-Kangas, T. (1981) *Bilingualism or Not. The Education of Minorities*. Clevedon: Multilingual Matters.

Vygotsky, L. S. (1978) *Mind in Society*. Cambridge, MA: Harvard University Press.

5 | 'Couldn't put Dumpy together again' – the significance of repetition and routine in young children's language development

Julia Gillen

Dumpy

I recently had to go on a long car journey with my three children, the oldest of whom is 6 years old. Many parents may sympathize with my increasingly desperate attempts to keep them amused with counting games, easy variants on the 'I spy' theme and so on, all fuelled by occasional snacks and drinks mostly of a horribly sugary nature. The most successful (i.e. long lasting) occupation was a game where we all had to sing nursery rhymes or little songs in turn.

My daughter Kathleen, who was then 2 years and 4 months old, sang 'Humpty Dumpty' every time it was her turn, for ten successive rounds. This was despite the fact she has a considerable, if not quite word-perfect repertoire of nursery rhymes acquired at nursery school and with her childminder. But each time she sang with gusto, making identical mistakes as follows:

> Humpy Dumpy sat on the wall
> All king's horses and all the king's men
> Couldn't put Dumpy together again

Her enjoyment in repeating this well-known rhyme has caused me to reflect on the place of this kind of behaviour in young children's growth in oral communication skills, and in turn to relate this to theoretical ideas about linguistic acquisition. In this chapter I want to argue for recognition of the importance of routine and repetition in young children's language development. I intend to link this to current controversies in the field of child language research and I hope thus provide backing for existing 'good practice'. Some practical observations I make might be new, especially for those fresh to the field of working with under-threes – or living with them! Chiefly, though, I suspect these ideas might be most useful as a stimulus for reflecting on why we do what we do, so that we can keep learning ourselves and improving our interactions with very young children.

But let me start with listening to Kathleen during that long journey through Scotland. I have already explained that through careful listening I noticed that she made exactly the same 'mistakes' each time. One fundamental distortion from the original is the omission of the second line altogether: 'Humpty Dumpty had a great fall.' She hasn't simply forgotten this on one occasion while trying to recite a half-remembered rhyme. Rather, she has created her own version which she repeats each time. Part of this version is her 'take' on the character's name. She always calls him 'Humpy Dumpy', missing off the *ts* consistently when reciting the first line. But the short form is always 'Dumpy'.

This is also how she refers to the character when speaking of it outside the rhyme situation. For example, when she wants her video of nursery rhymes on at home she always asks me to 'put Dumpy on'. This is clearly a creative language construction. Nobody ever named the nursery rhyme video by even a term close to this. Her father and I never called it the 'Humpty Dumpty video' but always 'the nursery rhyme video'. It was Kathleen who found her favourite nursery rhyme character the most memorable feature and therefore started to refer to the whole video simply as 'Dumpy'. Because she used this term when referring to the video in identical pragmatic situations, i.e. when it was clear to her parents by features of the physical context (place and timing) that she wanted a video on, this short term of hers functioned perfectly well, without ambiguity.

The request to 'put Dumpy on' has also been quite a repetitive one. Again, many carers will not be surprised to learn that in a certain place, i.e. her own living room, at certain times of the day and week it was quite a common phrase for some time. Other conjunctions of place and time which repeat themselves in her routine elicit other phrases used repetitively. Every time we drive past her nursery school she calls out 'my nursery school!'; then after I, or someone else in the car has agreed 'yes, it's your nursery school' she adds, 'Conor too big!' This statement then meets with agreement and usually expansion in which she takes considerable pleasure.

The origins of this regularly repeated game go back to when she first started attending nursery school, where she goes two days a week. At that time she was accompanied by her big brother Conor. But when he became 4 he started full-time at school (this being Lancashire). Trying to comfort Kathleen I tried to make something out of the fact that Conor and his peers were 'too big' to go, and that Kathleen and her friends were just the right size. This idea appealed to her; she soon developed the game, which the sight of the nursery school from the car rarely fails to trigger.

Some such routinized, repetitive language games of hers are not necessarily triggered off by certain conjunctions of circumstances. Just after her second birthday I was one day fiddling with the video trying to get something in particular to play. It might well have been 'Dumpy', for she was certainly paying attention and encouraging me! For a few seconds a television programme came onto the screen. The whole of the frame was filled by a small boy sticking his tongue out. Very shortly one of our videos came on, taking over. It wasn't the video I was looking for but rather a home-made one showing, again just for a few seconds, Kathleen's young cousin Morgan. I switched this off and continued my search. Meanwhile Kathleen was delighted. 'Boy! Naughty!' she said. 'Yes he was, wasn't he', I agreed. 'Boy stick tongue out!' she exclaimed, and again I agreed. 'Morgan!' was her next exclamation.

What surprised me about this was that even two weeks later she was quite often saying, quite out of the blue, 'Naughty boy! Stick tongue out!' with delight. I would generally agree. Then after a few seconds' pause she would say 'Morgan'. I had the idea she wasn't necessarily quite sure why she was saying it. Perhaps she could remember seeing Morgan's face just after that exciting incident, but somehow I felt that quite simply saying 'Morgan' had just become the next thing to say, like the next line in a re-created nursery rhyme. And what really surprised me about the episode is that even four months later she was still occasionally repeating the same phrases in full, like a mantra, even after long intervals such as two weeks in between instances. Unlike the examples discussed above, this particular language game was not provoked by repetitive triggers, at least as far as I could tell. On one occasion she suddenly began it while playing outdoors in a park.

I have established that for this particular child the use of routinized, repetitive phrases are part of what she does with language but, as surprising as it may seem, trying to relate this idea to theories about language in order, for example, to try to consider its significance, is to enter a minefield.

Chomsky and linguistics: no place for a child

I'll start by plunging into the greatest controversy in the study of language (in the industrialized 'western' world) of the twentieth century. This is centred around the ideas of Noam Chomsky and 'transformational grammar'. This is the study of the ways in which language is modified from its deep structure – in essence common to all languages – to the surface form in which it is found in any particular language. Chomsky's ideas have had such a profound impact on the study of language that I think it is interesting to examine something of their impact on child language research, both directly and indirectly.

When Noam Chomsky was invited to deliver a keynote address to the Boston University Child Language Conference in 1986 those present cannot have been much surprised by his characterization of all child language research as falling into one of three categories: wrong, trivial and absurd (Snow 1994: 4). Chomsky has long argued that the language a child hears continuously breaks the rules of the language: 'a good deal of normal speech consists of false starts, disconnected phrases and other distortions' (Chomsky 1967: 441).

We can probably all agree with Chomsky that virtually all children in normal circumstances acquire language and that they all learn it competently. Of course children will reach 'competence', however it might be measured, at different ages, but essentially the argument is that all children learn language unless they are prevented from doing so by specific handicaps or force of extreme circumstances. If we compare their command of language with other acquired skills, such as roller skating or piano playing, there is far less a degree of individual difference in the former. Therefore, according to the argument of Chomsky and his contemporary supporters, the crucial elements in our learning languages are innate: that is, we are all born with specific language-learning mechanisms. The interesting task then is to explore the structures that all languages have in common, that allow our inbuilt language-learning abilities to make sense of what we hear, and grasp what the true form of the language actually is.

It is important to note that many supporters and critics of Chomsky are concerned with language in a somewhat idealized, abstracted form. This suggests that for many linguists the language children use can be regarded as highly inferior. The example I gave above, 'Put Dumpy on', could be seen as structurally sound (reflecting a child's innate capabilities with syntax, according to Chomskian ideas) but highly situationally dependent. A listener, or reader of the sentence, needs to be provided with contextual information in order to understand it. It could therefore be characterized as inadequate whereas, as I argued above, it functions perfectly for Kathleen.

It is no accident, then, that to 'Linguistics' the study of child language acquisition is an isolated area of study, a very distinct research path. Theories of grammatical knowledge, of processing and of learning are generally seen as entirely separate, although there are in the 1990s a few researchers who are really only just beginning to propose a model of which they are different facets (Croft 1993).

A challenge to Chomsky: 'motherese' to child-directed speech

In the early 1970s the American academic Charles Ferguson became convinced of the value of modified registers for language learners. For example he characterized 'foreigner talk' as being a special way of speaking some people employed to make their language 'easier' in some respects and thus enable second language learners to participate more easily in conversations. He drew a parallel with 'motherese' – his term for the particular way mothers he had studied modified their speech when talking to young children.

The essential starting point in Ferguson and other associated linguists work has been a challenge to Chomsky's assertion that speech directed to children tends to be 'rather restricted in scope . . . and fairly degenerate in quality' (Chomsky 1965: 31). Rather, its new advocates argued that, in its special qualities, 'motherese' is designed to be helpful and beneficial to the young language learner. The overall aim of their research has been to define these qualities and prove the hypothesis that it is facilitative.

As this work developed the central term changed, firstly to 'baby talk', then to 'caregiver language'. These changes acknowledged that people other than mothers may be primary caregivers and then that others than primary caregivers may use this type of language. I will use the term 'child-directed speech' or CDS, in common with current usage, as for example by Gallaway and Richards (1994).

Here is a short example I overheard of Eamonn talking to his son Emlyn, who was 11 months old at the time: 'Come on then, shall we get you dressed? Shall we get you dressed?' The sentences are well structured and fairly simple. Although the first consists of two clauses, these are consecutive rather than embedded. There is entire repetition of one phrase used. The communication does not really have the function which study of the words alone might suggest, i.e. it is not really a question and Emlyn is not required to respond to the substance of the words (as considered from their 'semantic' function). Even the 'we' referred to is in fact Eamonn himself. But the sentences, and the calm, reassuring tone with which they are delivered are simply designed for their emotional affect. Emlyn is gradually learning that verbal announcements to do with getting dressed precede that particular activity, and he is being reassured so that he will not be negatively surprised by the experience.

The qualities of CDS as recognized today are discussed by Pine (1994). There are differences in every aspect of speech. Utterances tend to consist of short, well-formed sentences or phrases. There are fewer false starts or hesitations than in speech otherwise, presumably partly just because of the extra simplicity. The voice tends to be pitched higher, intonation is exaggerated and often tempo is slowed down. The content involves repetitions, is highly tied to the here and now (for example what the child is doing) and is to a high degree 'redundant' i.e. not all the words are necessary if the communication is regarded in terms of its semantic meaning. Furthermore CDS 'employs a number of special discourse features which serve to involve the child in interaction and to clarify and upgrade the child's own contribution' (Pine 1994: 15).

These features may thus include echoes of what the child has said (or non-verbally contributed perhaps). These may be expanded, perhaps by suggesting a verbal interpretation of a non-verbal contribution even in consciousness of doubtful validity, for example if Emlyn's answering smile is interpreted as agreement to his father's proposal and Eamonn says, 'That's all right with you then.' Or perhaps a brief word or two by a child is expanded into a full sentence, or turned into a question back to them. The aim of this behaviour, as Pine suggests, would seem to be to include and encourage the child, while providing them with models.

Ochs (1986) points out that announcements to children about what is about to happen are often used in order to assist the child to understand what is going on and/or suggest to them what they should do next, or indeed *not* do next. This is very likely the true communicative function for Eamonn's utterance: to provide some information and, above all, reassurance: don't get upset, do be helpful if you can.

I have alluded to many features of CDS and I would not want to suggest that all of these are present in every utterance directed to a young child. But at the same time I suggest that it is a recognizable phenomenon in, at least, English-speaking western culture.

An enormous number of studies into CDS have been carried out over the last 20 years or so, as reported in Gallaway and Richards (1994). For every study that has suggested some link between some feature of CDS and a positive feature of infant or child language acquisition, a challenge has often arisen. This is mainly because it is very difficult to isolate a particular feature (let us say the shortness of sentences), and prove that it is a significant factor. However, this has been a fascinating area for research over the last two decades, with much ingenious methodology being contrived (Snow 1994).

What can be learned from cross-cultural research

Even if we are tempted to believe in the original 'motherese' hypothesis (i.e. that CDS is facilitative), a challenge has come from studying how children learn language in very different cultural surroundings. In Samoa, for example, the very idea of adapting one's language to the child is unthinkable because people of lower status (for example children) have to make adjustments to those of higher status (Ochs 1982). Among the Kaluli of New Guinea, caregivers will not talk to children in the first few months of life. However, they will hold up babies to others, such as siblings, and talk as if for the baby in a high-pitched voice. Later, young children are explicitly taught certain language constructions, such as certain forms of teasing (Schieffelin 1986). Cross-cultural research, then, has shown that CDS (as known in English-speaking Anglo-American society) is most certainly not a requisite for language learning, and that children can get on just as well without it.

How? Elena Lieven is a psychologist in child language research who is also very interested in findings from cross-cultural research (Lieven 1994). She poses a very interesting idea. A function of some features of CDS, it is argued effectively by some researchers, is to help prelinguistic infants to begin to 'segment speech through stress patterns, which emphasise content words, longer pauses between clause boundaries, etc.' (p. 61). It is well known that ordinary verbal speech flows over and through words; we do not speak staccato, with our breaks conveniently between words. It seems convincing to argue that the slower tempo, repetition of content and intonational contours of CDS are facilitative in allowing the very young to begin to come to understanding. But in cultures which do not have specific CDS, children actively carry out this segmentation for themselves. In one society infants begin talking by echoing the ends of utterances they overhear in adult conversation. It is common also to begin talking by producing 'unanalysed, rote-learned segments which they have picked up in routinised situations' (p. 62). The repetition of these 'frozen phrases' can then lead to their segmentation and analysis. Thus from being capable of using them with limited or even no understanding, the child gradually becomes capable of both deeper understanding and more productive, even creative manipulation of those phrases, for example adapting them to slightly different situations, and/or with some appropriate variation.

I think that apart from the work of Lieven (1994) and Peters and Boggs (1986) there has been little recognition of the importance of such means of learning to children in our society by those who ascribe great significance to the qualities of the sociocultural environment in the language-learning process.

I would like to try to follow Lieven, or at least my interpretation of her work, and argue for the importance and significance of the repetition of speech routines and repetition within a view (sometimes termed 'social constructivist') of child language development that acknowledges the shaping force of society as well as the individual creative activity of the child.

What precisely do I mean here by a speech routine? I follow Peters and Boggs (1986) in asserting that they vary in degree of fixity. If someone says 'Knock, knock' they will expect the exact response 'Who's there?' But more common are somewhat looser formulae such as, 'What is that?' expecting either 'That's a . . .' or simply the name of the object, or perhaps 'I don't know.' The point is that a limited number of types of responses are expected and found, at least on the vast majority of occasions. The phrases in this type of routine are sometimes termed 'slot and fill'.

These routines are part of our social knowledge. Learning language is inextricably tied with socialization; as children learn to participate in social events they are learning what kinds of things are said at the same time as they are learning about the roles and relationships of the participants. Different societies will have different customs in language as in all else, and will inculcate their youngest into common patterns, more or less fixed, of speech routines.

I will try, then, to support my claim that repetition of speech routines is as significant a part of language development in our society as any other, regardless of the presence or absence of CDS, from observations of two different kinds of routinized behaviour in the under-threes: politeness rituals and play with toy telephones.

Politeness rituals

Kathleen attends a day nursery two days a week. This is a privately run centre comprising three units: one for babies aged between 1 and 2 years old; a 'Tweeny room' for children aged 2 to 3 1/2 and then the 'Big room' for the remaining children until they begin school. (In this area, children who are 4 years old on 1 September begin school full-time during the preceding August.) I have made a few visits to the nursery over the last couple of years, on days when Kathleen and/or Conor have not been present in order to make certain research observations; naturally I also make visits when they are there in a purely parental capacity! I have been warmly welcomed whatever the reason for my visit by the owner/manager and her staff.

So I was in the 'Baby room' one November morning when five children (four from 12 to 14 months old and one 2-year-old visitor from the 'Tweeny room') received their snacks – a drink and biscuit. As each snack was put on the small table in front of each child the adult said 'Ta' in a friendly but deliberate way, in a clearly routine effort at trying to teach the child to say 'ta'. A few minutes later I was in the Tweeny room while a similar ritual was enacted for those children, this time sitting in small groups around tables. This time the children were supposed to say 'thank you'; or, if they did not, again they received the prompt, 'thank you'.

I think this is a fairly unremarkable teaching of politeness skills; I doubt that anyone, parents, other carers, etc. would think it anything but welcome if they thought about it at all. Yet reflection shows that it is very culture-specific. In Japan, politeness is a complex matter entailing a lot of indirect speech and a considerable set of politeness 'markers' (such as, in English, 'please'). Japanese mothers teach culturally required skills of politeness, for example by speaking 'for' others, who might not have said anything, or by diverting children from socially inappropriate direct requests by themselves making an indirect response, and modelling the politeness markers (Clancy 1986). On the other hand a Spanish friend visiting me when Kathleen was 21 months old found it amazing that my daughter would say (at meal time) 'please', 'thank you' and even 'thank you much'. According to my visitor, Spanish children would not learn such politeness markers until much later, and no one would dream of trying to instil them at such an early age.

Lieven observes that explicit teaching of politeness routines, often studied in cross-cultural, mainly anthropological research, also does occur in western society but is rarely noted, 'perhaps because it is regarded as not very important, at least in the groups usually studied, and also because it is relatively simple' (Lieven 1994: 65). I think this is a case of familiarity leading to a certain cultural blindness. In actual fact some of Kathleen's early language speech exchanges were directly taught (at least some of the time) modelled (again at least some of the time), and were learned through the use of repetition of formulaic phrases in routinized, even ritualized situations. To an observer coming from a position of a 'less polite' speech community than ours, rather than one used to observing or considering observations of societies with more complex politeness systems, the strength of the cultural values which were leading to that form of politeness inculcation in a young child's early speech was strongly marked and clearly effective.

Toy telephones

I am a member of the Telephone Project at the Manchester Metropolitan University – a research project directed by Nigel Hall and Rob Greenall investigating children's language behaviour with telephones.

Part of our work is concerned with children playing with toy telephones. Observations have been collected in a number of settings. With the under-threes most of the data has been collected in homes, often by myself. When a little girl called Nadia, aged 2 years 5 months, was visiting my house, she picked up a toy telephone and said, 'Hello hello bye see you later', and then put the phone down. She had picked out formulaic openings and endings in her pretence phone call. Others have noticed this tendency in young children to use formulaic utterances when they first start playing on the telephone. Ervin-Tripp (reported in Peters and Boggs 1986: 83) recorded an 18-month-old as saying, 'Hi fine bye.'

One of our studies of 3- and 4-year-old children in a nursery setting demonstrated that 71 per cent of the children's calls began with a 'correct opening', usually 'hello'. 'Yes, who is it?' was also deemed a 'correct opening' when the child was evidently playing at answering an incoming call (Gillen 1995). It seems from this and current work that it is the use of these repetitive, formulaic utterances, which presumably they have often overheard from listening to one end of a conversation, that young children first pick up on when starting off in this type of play. (To see some of the fascinating channels their play then diversifies into, see Hall *et al.* 1996.)

Conclusions

I have tried to combine both theoretical ideas from child language research and wider language studies with evidence from practice to support my argument that repetition of speech routines is important in children's language development. I will try to put forward some practical suggestions to encourage those working with young children under 3 to consider.

Firstly, it could perhaps be useful to think about the following issues:

- Do you think you modify your language when talking with the children?
- If so, in what ways do you think you do this? How do you think the children benefit? (It might be useful to have someone else observe you and help you work out answers here.)
- Do you provide the children with opportunities for structured language routines – for example by means of a 'register ritual', the use of nursery rhymes and so on.
- Are children provided with stimulus toys that encourage the enactment of routines, such as toy telephones or dressing-up clothes?
- Finally, why not join the great debate? To what extent, if any, do you think children's language acquisition is innate?

I will now discuss observations of good practice in connection with two activities regularly present in educare settings. I consider relevant sites for practice of repetitive routines in language development: toy telephones and nursery rhymes.

Toy telephones

For young children under 3, these seem to be most often placed just like any other toy, in a box or collection of toys from which children can self-select. However, comparing how they are often made available in nursery settings for 3- to 4-year-olds, it might be of interest to consider whether these opportunities might be worth considering for younger children as well.

I have seen toy telephones presented in two distinctly different ways in nursery settings for 3- to 4-year-olds. The first, and most common in my experience, is to place the telephone in a setting designed to enhance pretence play. For example if the telephone is sited in a 'home corner', pretence calls to parents and carers often result. Calls to doctors and the emergency services are also often stimulated, especially if appropriate dressing-up clothes are provided. I have argued elsewhere that in these calls children can demonstrate and practise developing skills of register (i.e. appropriate and differentiated ways of speaking) when playing at particular roles in certain contexts (Gillen 1996). Especially perhaps with older children, siting the telephone in a shop, cafe or other such more complex setting may encourage different appropriate communicative strategies to be used.

Secondly, I have seen toy telephones deliberately placed in a book corner. For young children, looking at books is likely to encourage talk, perhaps to oneself while 'reading'. (This relates to the 'emergent literacy' perspective, see for example Barratt-Pugh, Chapter 3.) Toy telephones may well encourage similar behaviour, i.e. the child talks 'for themselves': therefore it is sensible to put them near the books.

Nursery rhymes

Finally, much research has been carried out into nursery rhymes: they have been associated with developing phonological skills (Bryant 1989); leading into reading (Bryant 1989; Marriott 1992); second language learning and acculturation (Klippel 1990); the appreciation of rhythm and physical development (Wetton 1981); and the obvious route into music. It is time that the centrality of developing oracy in young children (and the expertise involved) be accorded greater recognition, for example through specialist training opportunities.

I therefore include here as a final section an account by Mrs Boyle, an educare worker with the under-threes, who is an expert practitioner with nursery rhymes, songs and music. She has many years' experience and is a much-loved member of the local community. She is currently working as morning manager of the Baby room in the nursery school which Kathleen attends. When she walks near the local school she is often greeted affectionately by those she used to look after; in some cases these are now the parents of her current charges!

> I'm in charge of the Baby room (for 1- to 2-year-olds) during the mornings. I also keep in contact with the children as they move into the Tweeny room (2- to 3-year olds) and the Big room (for 3-year-olds and over, until starting school at 4). I'm one of the first people here in the morning from 7.15 a.m., and from then until 8.00 a.m. I'm with all the children who are here that early. We give the children toast and juice. Then I also spend some time with the older ones doing music, for example practising for the Christmas show.
>
> At eight o'clock we come with the 'babies' – the two or three who are here by that time – into the Baby room. Three or four of the tweenies ask to come in as well. Occasionally, especially soon after they've made the move they might spend half their day or more in here but generally it's just for ten minutes or so. They'll get me to put a tape on the cassette player and for a while it's singing and dancing. No matter how young they are they love to dance.

Later in the morning, just before snack time, we'll have ten minutes sitting down and singing nursery rhymes and other songs. In September we have all new ones and for the first couple of months they're just enjoying themselves and starting to join in the actions. After a couple of months they'll all be singing. By the time they're 2 they'll be much noisier and joining in everything: when we sing 'If you're happy and you know it say "we are!"' they really raise the roof. If you go and see them in the Tweeny room you'll see they all like singing and choosing themselves which songs to sing.

Last year I realized that the 'babies' – they were coming up to 2 years old then – were singing for the last line of 'Baa Baa Black Sheep': 'and one for Mrs Barlow who lives down the lane' – it must have sounded the same! [Mrs Barlow is the owner-manager of the nursery school.]

My granddaughter teaches me a lot of rhymes new to me such as 'Little Mousie Brown'. I also make up my own songs, rhymes and stories. I started doing that when I had some eye trouble and couldn't see to read easily. I started making up stories for the big ones – and they preferred the ones I told to stories from books. I couldn't remember them from one year to another and so I started writing them down. I also write songs and we sing them for the Christmas show and occasions like that. I like being with the older children for singing but I do like working with the babies.

What I personally find most important about her account is the way that the use of nursery rhymes is incorporated in a philosophy of childcare that emphasizes their creativity and powers of enjoyment, particularly in music. She indirectly contends that making a place for repetition and routine in children's development is certainly not an argument for a return to old-fashioned rote learning, but rather that it can be incorporated in a holistic, child-centred approach to educare. It is time that nursery rhymes and other vehicles through which children learn language with enjoyment were taken seriously – by us that is, not the children. Three cheers for Dumpy!

Suggestions for further reading

If you would like to read more about child language research, I recommend these very accessible books:

Crystal, D. (1986) *Listen to Your Child*. Harmondsworth: Penguin.
   A very entertaining read as well as informative and stimulating.
Peccei, J. Stilwell (1994) *Child Language*. London: Routledge.
   This is a simple and lucid introduction to the current state of knowledge.

References

Bryant, P. E. (1989) Nursery rhymes, phonological skills and reading, *Journal of Child Language*, 16(2): 407–28.

Chomsky, N. (1965) *Aspects of the Theory of Syntax*. Cambridge, MA: MIT Press.

Chomsky, N. (1967) The formal nature of language, in E. H. Lenneberg (ed.) *Biological Foundations of Language*. New York: Wiley.

Clancy, P. (1986) The acquisition of communicative style in Japanese, in B. Schieffelin and E. Ochs (eds) *Language Socialization Across Cultures*. New York: Cambridge University Press.

Croft, W. (1993) What are the connections? Language acquisition and linguistic theory, in E. Clark (ed.) *The Proceedings of the 25th Child Language Research Forum*. Stanford: Center for the Study of Language and Information, Leland Stanford Junior University.

Gallaway, C. and Richards, B. (eds) (1994) *Input and Interaction in Language Acquisition*. Cambridge: Cambridge University Press.

Gillen, J. (1995) '"It's for you Daddy!" A linguistic analysis of young children's learning during episodes of pretence play with a toy telephone', unpublished MA in Education thesis, Open University.

Gillen, J. (1996) The development of young children's ability to use the language of telephone discourse. Conference paper, British Educational Research Association Annual Conference, 12 September.

Hall, N., Gillen, J. and Greenall, R. (1996) 'Don't cry, I ring the cop shop': young children's pretend telephone behaviours, in N. Hall and J. Martello (eds) *Listening to Children Think: Exploring Talk in the Early Years*. London: Hodder and Stoughton.

Heath, S. B. (1983) *Ways with Words: Language, Life and Work in Communities and Classrooms*. Cambridge: Cambridge University Press.

Klippel, F. (1990) From nursery rhymes to TV documentaries, *Language Learning Journal*, 1: 58–62.

Lieven, E. (1994) Crosslinguistic and crosscultural aspects of language addressed to children, in C. Gallaway and B. Richards (eds) *Input and Interaction in Language Acquisition*. Cambridge: Cambridge University Press.

Marriott, S. (1992) Reading pictures: children's responses to nursery rhymes, *Education 3–13*, 20(3): 39–44.

Ochs, E. (1982) Talking to children in Western Samoa, *Language in Society*, 11: 77–104.

Ochs, E. (1986) Introduction, in B. Schieffelin and E. Ochs (eds) *Language Socialization across Cultures*. New York: Cambridge University Press.

Peters, A. M. and Boggs, S. T. (1986) Interactional routines as cultural influences upon language acquisition, in B. Schieffelin and E. Ochs (eds) *Language Socialization across Cultures*. New York: Cambridge University Press.

Pine, J. (1994) The language of primary caregivers, in C. Gallaway and B. Richards (eds) *Input and Interaction in Language Acquisition*. Cambridge: Cambridge University Press.

Schieffelin, B. B. (1986) Teasing and shaming in Kaluli children's interactions, in B. Schieffelin and E. Ochs (eds) *Language Socialization across Cultures*. New York: Cambridge University Press.

Snow, C. E. (1994) Introduction – beginning from baby talk: twenty years of research on input in interaction, in C. Gallaway and B. Richards (eds) *Input and Interaction in Language Acquisition*. Cambridge: Cambridge University Press.

Wetton, P. (1981) Nursery rhymes and rhythm, *Action*, 12(4): 100–1.

6 | 'It's a princess' – fostering creative and aesthetic development in young children

Hilary Renowden

Introduction

'That's a nice cake', said the well-meaning adult as Francesca held up her lump of pink playdough with a feather stuck on the top and sequins pressed into it – 'It's a princess!', said Francesca.

The above incident, recorded some time ago, had a profound effect on my subsequent response to young children's creative expression. I came to realize just how far insensitive handling of young children's early creative experiences can have a profound effect on later learning, and how careful observation of young children and sensitive involvement of adults, can become an essential tool in diagnosing and assessing young children's needs and abilities.

The focus of this book is on early interactions and particularly on the interactions between adults and very young children. The Rumbold Report (DES 1990) presents a formidable list of areas of knowledge, skills and attitudes required by adults who have responsibility for young children's learning and development. Nutbrown (1996: 54) re-emphasizes the point that 'adult knowledge is crucial to extending children's learning and essential if children's early achievements are to be recognised and respected'. I came to realize that knowledge about the process of learning is just as important as knowledge about the child. All adults who work with children under 3 have a tremendous responsibility to engage in the kinds of positive interactions which foster free expression of interest, skill, ability and emotion.

It is argued that providing children with opportunities to explore the world from an early age and to express their true emotions as they react to a range of experiences and interactions, has a powerful effect on intellectual development. Goleman (1996) argues that the rules which govern emotions and therefore condition intelligence can be acquired early in life at the hands of a skilled adult. He believes strongly that educators should provide for the emotional and creative – as well as the academic education – of children. 'All emotions are, in essence, impulses to act, the instant plans for handling life that evolution has instilled in us . . . In the dance of feeling and thought the emotional faculty guides our moment-to-moment decisions, working hand in hand with the rational mind, enabling – or disabling – thought itself' (Goleman 1996: 34).

Early interactions with skilled and knowledgeable adults are crucial for healthy emotional development. The building of relationships between adults and children is an important and sensitive area. Vygotsky (1978) stressed the crucial role of the adult in young children's learning, emphasizing the need to 'be around' in order to help the child cope effectively in what he termed the 'zone of proximal development'. This he describes as the gap between what a child can do with help 'today' and what unaided, but with appropriate support, she will be able to do tomorrow.

Nutbrown (1996) refers to the importance of 'adults seeing with wide eyes and open minds', for after all, isn't this the way in which young children learn? She argues that children have an awesome capacity to observe in fine detail and they learn from what they see. One of the main problems in this busy world in which we are always hurrying children on to the next stage or even to the next activity, is that we do not give children sufficient time to observe the world in fine detail.

For children under 3 this opportunity is particularly important. Not only are they absorbing a wealth of new information but they are constantly adapting their thinking in order to make sense of this new knowledge about the world and the people and objects around them. The balance between these twin processes, which Piaget (1951) termed assimilation and accommodation, are essential for effective learning, but the process requires understanding, patience and time on the part of adults.

I believe that this is particularly important in relation to creative and aesthetic development. In approaching early learning with 'wide eyes and open minds' Nutbrown argues that 'educators need to respond with sensitivity and respect to what they see'. Communication between parents and educators and continuity of experience between home and group settings is all-important. 'Respectful observation can occur where the climate is such that educators and parents – together – watch, listen to and talk with children' (Nutbrown 1996: 83).

The role of parents, as first educators of their child, cannot be overemphasized. A rich visually stimulating home environment complements and reinforces the experiences provided in the nursery or day care setting. Even during the first few months of life children exposed to an enriched visual environment develop faster than children who do not have anything interesting or stimulating on which to focus. Bronfenbrenner (1968) argued that children raised in an atmosphere of sterility and deprivation fall behind their more advantaged peers in all phases of their growth. Bradley *et al.* (1979) found that the competence of children between 12 and 24 months of age increased when parents encouraged and challenged their abilities. The interaction between children and their environment is a crucial element in early learning. The snapshots which follow capture some of those interactions between under-threes in my nursery and the environment which I have been careful to preserve for them. A group of young children, their ages ranging between 1 year and 4 years 3 months are happily playing in the field surrounding the nursery. Their teacher observing them writes:

The field
The field is a carpet of gold, white and green – dandelions, buttercups and daisies. The sun is shining and the children open the gate and run into this golden haze. They laugh, squeal with delight, others sit down, touch, look, in private groups of twos and threes, some roll over, lie in the mass of flowers, while others sit and stare. How rare an experience it is just to be able to sit in a field full of flowers, to watch the bees and insects busy flitting from flower to flower and just to *be*. To experience freedom, happiness and *joy*. Nature is one continuing miracle with which children are at one. Hopefully these experiences so early in life help to instil an awareness of beauty and the realization of just how precious it is.

Wild flowers
We leave patches of lawn to grow into long grass. There are lovely varieties of wild flowers: from the carpet of daisies and buttercups which the children run through, to the yellow dandelions we collect and make into dandelion 'crowns' which we proudly wear. We collect and pick very carefully the dandelion clocks and we're shown how to blow them gently and watch the seeds 'like parachutes' land in the grass, or be carried off by the wind. We collect handfuls of golden, shining buttercups, some of us end up collecting small fistfuls of the shiny heads, these are carefully placed in vases to go on the lunch table, or to float on bowls of water. The children can count the petals, be aware of the beauty of the colour, examine their own pollen-covered fingers and make and wear daisy chains. How many fields do we see today with wild flowers in? How many wild flowers do the children see? To live and sit in long grass surrounded by them, to become aware of the world of small insects and creatures we see scurrying up and down stems and along the ground as we sit quietly and watch – ladybirds, spiders, caterpillars, greenfly – so many. This awareness, I believe, must be given to each child early in life, it is of such value for the rest of its life. It encourages a true sensitivity of nature and nature's gifts of which we are only a small part, but of equal importance to all life's cycle. We have so much power to protect and cultivate or destroy. I believe this starts at a very early age.

What were those children learning as they played in the field?

This is the question with which early childhood educators are continuously faced and it is no less important for those working with the under-threes. It could be argued that the children were gaining a wide range of curriculum experience. If asked to draw a flowchart in order to illustrate their learning it might appear as shown in Figure 6.1.

But what were the children really learning? Accepting that this kind of experience is available to all young children, what of their creative, aesthetic and emotional development? Much has been written about creativity and the importance of the adults in harnessing the child's natural curiosity and interest and building on that first-hand experience – what is often referred to as 'capturing the un-returning moment'. For those children, and for the adult watching them in that field, that was an 'un-returning moment'.

Social skills
Being part of a pair/group
Sharing
Emotional experience
Playing together
Confident use of space

Maths
Sets of different flowers, grasses
Counting
Sorting
Discrimination
Recognizing shape, colour, size

Initial stimulus
Playing in a field of wild flowers, tall grass

Language
Descriptive
Experiences
Verbal and non-verbal
Communicating feeling and sharing stories, rhymes
Songs
Recall memory

Science
Insects, flowers
Needs for growth – rain, sun, soil
Homes of insects
Recognizing parts of a flower
Observing changing weather and seasons

Creative and aesthetic
Sensual experience
Colours
Textures
Creative activities: paints, pastels, pens, collages, clay, etc.

Figure 6.1 Learning in the field

These first-hand experiences are possible for all children: going out in the rain with wellies on, splashing in a puddle, running over the yard watching their footprints dry, making kites and watching them rise in the wind, or touching the bark on a tree and the brightly coloured tulip brought in by the teacher/carer. These experiences are made possible by knowledgeable and skilful carers and teachers of very young children, and their understanding of what children are observing and absorbing from these experiences. I am now in the enviable position of being able to share those early experiences with the children for whom I am responsible.

In the local infant/nursery school of which I was previously head teacher, and in most of the other schools I have worked in during the last 30 years, it was becoming more and more difficult to fit these vital first-hand experiences into the curriculum – in the latter years, impossible. In 1989 I took early retirement, disillusioned and exhausted as head of a school on a socially disadvantaged estate where jobs had failed to materialize. Coping with limited resources, endless bureaucracy and red tape, there was little time for the individual's needs, for flexibility within the curriculum and so little *time*. Finding it impossible to compromise my values and philosophy with regard to the education of the very young child, I decided not to continue.

After a year's rest in which I recharged my batteries and reflected on my beliefs, my enthusiasm and commitment to the early years returned and I decided to open my own nursery based upon the day care/nurseries I had studied and visited in Scandinavia in the 1980s. The emphasis was on a non-institutionalized, child-centred environment, with a strong underlying structure. Importance was placed as equally on the environment and outdoor resources as on the resources indoors, with natural materials being used wherever possible. Indoors full-sized tables, real paintings, wallpaper and curtains all help to create a warm and welcoming environment. All play and creative materials are housed/stored on open shelves and are accessible to children throughout the day. This accessibility from an early age encourages choice, respect and self-discipline as well as nurturing independence and creative expression. Outside there is sand, water, a mud pie area, all manner of 'dens', a large tarmac yard, a children's raised flower and vegetable garden, a large field with a special conservation area designed by the older children and much loved by the youngest 'crawlies' who will crawl the width of the field to get to it! We also have chickens, rabbits, guinea pigs, ducks and two nursery cats. There are taps and sinks (at the children's height) outside, and lots of wooden equipment, which lends itself to fantasy, imaginative role play.

The nursery caters for 78 children from 4 months to 5 years each week, with 20 per cent attending full-time. Staff range from full-time nursery nurses to 50-year-old 'grans', who all have a different role to play within the nursery and are chosen for their special qualities in addition to their qualifications. The staff ratio is 1:5 for the over-twos, 1:3 for the under-twos and babies under 6 months have a 1:1 carer. The children in the nursery school are highly motivated and their paintings, drawings and writings add to their growing powers of confidence and self-expression.

I strongly believe that it is important to develop creativity at an early age and agree with Lowenfeld and Brittain (1987: 91) that 'creative attitudes, i.e. finding the unknown challenging, coming up with unique thoughts and ideas, looking for differences and similarities and having interesting thoughts and attitudes are established early in life and are likely to continue'.

Providing opportunities for babies and very young children to attend the nursery allowed me to observe and support their creative development from an early age and to put my philosophy into practice. This includes the following aims and considerations:

- to create an environment as close to a home as possible;
- to give high quality care/educational experiences;
- to employ mature staff chosen, in particular, for their qualities in working alongside parents;
- to ensure that each baby and its parents will relate to two key people;
- to ensure that each baby/child will be treated as an individual, precious 'being', developing her own personality and having her individual needs met in appropriate ways;
- for parents to have access, support and confidence in the staff and be responsible in as many ways as possible for their baby's needs;
- to provide and maintain an environment which is exciting and stimulating as well as being natural and caring, adult to child, child to adult, child to child, all to the environment;
- to provide opportunities for all children to develop this awareness of and respect for all things, a natural curiosity, and to provide every opportunity and experience to encourage healthy development in all areas – language, social, physical, emotional;
- to avoid plastic, garish materials and to use natural materials. To prepare natural, wholesome, fresh food, daily;
- to take every opportunity to foster and support the child's early, creative expression and interest;
- to have time to listen, time to talk and time to *be*.

My beliefs about young children's creative development have grown out of my experience of working alongside and observing them, seeing them respond even as tiny babies to the environment of people, things, objects, flowers and animals, and watching them develop emotionally, socially and creatively.

I have also been influenced by what I have read, by research into the ways in which young children learn and develop. I feel that it is very important to nurture creative expression in young babies from birth. Observing babies closely, as Goldschmied and Selleck (1996) demonstrate in their excellent videos, shows the adult just how capable young babies are. The adults' responsibility is to offer a rich and appropriate range of stimulating opportunities for interactions and to allow children to demonstrate their creative abilities.

Very young babies learn and explore through the senses. This nurtures creative development; during these early months all experiences are being absorbed and the pathways from senses to brain are becoming well defined.

Babies are totally dependent upon adults to provide for their experiences and development until they become mobile. If babies are left unattended, ignored, with little stimulation, they quickly become bored, distressed or complacent. When their needs are met, with freedom of movement, stimulation, rich experiences, curiosity encouraged and nurtured they naturally progress and demand more, always progressing, learning and discovering through their senses.

Creative expression is an intrinsic part of every human being and it cannot be separated into compartments or contained and defined by boundaries. It has no beginning and no end. It is the source, or the self, and can be called a life force or life energy. Curiosity leads to development. I believe that it is wondrous, miraculous, individual and unique to each of us how we interpret, store and express our experiences and feelings.

It can, however, be stifled, crushed, abused, ignored, belittled, underestimated or undervalued but, there is no denying that it exists. Babies who have been contained, controlled and 'adult-programmed' are examples of this. In severe conditions this can result in apathy, head-banging, rocking and switching off from life. Babies/toddlers who have experienced this but in less extreme forms are often described as a 'good baby', happy sitting in her/his high chair/playpen, and causing little trouble.

When observing very young babies exposed to an interesting, stimulating environment, they seem to be part of this creative life energy. Adults must be sensitive as this process is evolving, to understand babies'/toddlers' needs and provide the environment and stimulus to encourage and enable these sensual experiences and then to nurture them.

The changes that take place in children's creative expression are a direct reflection of the changing child; Lowenfeld and Brittain (1987) argue that all of the variables that cause them to be different individuals with different personalities and interests also influence their creative products. In the case of children under 3 their earliest 'products' reflect their first attempts to make sense of and to interpret and represent the world as they see it (see, for example, Figure 6.2). At any level we cannot understand a work of art unless we understand the culture in which it was produced, the artist's intentions, and the society and environmental conditions that surround its making. The same holds true for young children's creative expression: the environment, the intent of the child, the intellectual and emotional factors involved – all must be understood if we are to appreciate and develop their early creative endeavours.

The role of the adult in engaging with the child in early interactions is crucial not only in the development of art but of the children themselves. It is only through a strongly supportive adult who encourages and interacts with children that an increased sensitivity towards the environment can grow.

Lowenfeld and Brittain assert that 'it is only through the senses that learning can take place' and that

> people seem to be relying less and less on actual sensory contact with their environment. They are becoming passive viewers of their culture rather than active makers of it . . . Touching, seeing, hearing, smelling

and tasting involve the active participation of the individual. There is evidence that even the young child needs to be truly encouraged to see, touch or become involved in the environment.

(Lowenfeld and Brittain 1987: 11 and 13)

The following examples reflect the ways in which very young children make sense of their environment and respond to it.

Oliver (5 months) has been in the nursery from the age of 4 months. Lying on the floor with his nappy off, feet and legs bare, he has lots of interaction with adults and other children, lots of freedom of movement, he is exposed to environment outside and inside, natural, sensual experiences.

At nappy changing he was given different objects to hold: a small piece of driftwood, shiny spoon, sponge, etc. to turn and look at. A mirror was positioned alongside the changing mat so that he could turn his head and see himself. He would lie on a fluffy mat, a satin sheet, a piece of rubber underlay, you could see his facial expressions – interested, curious, sensually aware of different textures, exploring with fingers and feet.

When he could be propped up (4–5 months) he was given a 'treasure basket' (Goldschmied 1987). He chose a shiny jam lid, ran his fingers over the shiny surface looking closely at the reflected lights, the shape, smoothness, feeling coldness in his mouth with his fingers turning it round, upside

Figure 6.2 Megan draws her family and writes her name at the top

down, concentrating, absorbed completely in this sensual experience. One could almost visualize the transmission going on between hands, eyes, brain – reinforcing pathways, absorbing information – reliving experiences in non-verbal terms.

Gabriella (10 months) sits in the autumn leaves watching them rustle and move for quite a while then puts out her hand to touch. They move – a brown, yellow and green mass moving quickly, she picks a fistful up and brings it near to look closely, then holds her fist out and lets them drift and fall back through the space. She repeats this over and over, observing colour, texture, movement and sound also becoming aware of space. (Many adults might intervene – not allowing the experience because they are pre-programmed with what they expect babies to do, i.e. put leaves in the mouth.)

Ellie (12 weeks) is unable to sit up or explore other than her immediate environment. She is dependent upon the adults in her day to provide her with stimuli and experiences. A feather mobile is one of her favourites. It is made up of exotic coloured feathers that move in the breeze. Adults blow it and Ellie imitates. She lies outside, under the trees in her pram with children's laughter all around. When carried outside she licks, chuckles, touches, smells.

Jack (12 months) sits among stones and pebbles. He studies them closely, lifting them up one at a time and placing them back carefully, then places them in different positions very carefully and with 'order'.

Megan (15 months) tentatively looks at the wet paint being poured onto the table. She moves away, watches from a distance as the adult puts her fingers in and moves and slides them about. The adult sits down by the table and draws Megan within the circle of her arm towards the table. She watches other children but does not want to touch the paint herself. Only when the adult moves away does she touch it with one finger; then she goes a bit further until she's got her whole palm in, moving it round. Soon she is lost in the experience, smoothing, sliding the wet, coloured liquid, making patterns with her fingers and eventually asking others to 'Look, look!'

Emily (9 months) is very alert and receptive to all stimuli present to her. We put her to sit on the grass outside in the garden. She cautiously puts out her hand and touches the grass, quickly withdrawing it, then looks closely at all this new green 'prickly stuff!' She gingerly touches it again and again with her palm outstretched, looking attentively now. Her socks are removed and immediately she moves her feet, spreads her toes out and moves them in the grass, feeling the texture as she did with her hands. Emily then grasps a piece of grass, pulls and brings it up to her face, looks intently at her tight fist with green stems sticking out then lets it go. She repeats this several times. Emily then sees the white flowers (daisies). She reaches over and touches them, then grasps the head and does the same as she did with the grass.

She was absorbed completely in her sensual activity, first sensitively feeling the soft, springing, cool grass. The sensations as she moved her feet in the grass (all being absorbed and stored in her brain) and her concentration as she picks a flower head off and intently studies it before getting another.

The under-twos unit was designed specifically as an open plan unit. Very young babies have an area open to the main room; for their safety a movable rail separates them from the more mobile toddlers. When they are lying or sitting they are able to see and interact with the other children. Babies spend a great deal of time outside sitting, crawling or walking in the garden among their older 'colleagues'. They spend a lot of time watching and imitating the older children.

As soon as they can crawl and stand they are able to mix with the older children in the unit, experiencing the delights of water, sand, painting and all creative activities. The 2-year-olds integrate with the older children in the nursery school for all outside activities and can wander in and out of both units, partaking in all activities and experiences.

There are dangers in separating age groups for long periods of time, and although young babies and toddlers need a safe and more protected environment it is essential that they be a part of the whole nursery and do not become an isolated unit. A recent study (Abbott *et al.* 1996) looks at the need for young babies to observe and be part of a mixed age group. As soon as they are mobile, the study suggests, given the freedom they are off in search of new stimulating pastures – as Oliver at 15 months demonstrates.

Oliver makes his way out of the baby unit, across the yard where all the children are playing – on he walks on his fat, chubby legs, purposefully towards the nursery school. He is going to the drawing table. I follow unobtrusively behind. He goes through the door, manoeuvres himself up the step, through the cloakroom into the lounge, climbs on a chair and reaches towards the penholder. Here he deliberately selects a green felt-tipped pen, pulls the lid off which takes quite an effort, gets a piece of paper from the paper box and draws. He stops to watch some older children walk in, then carries on drawing circular scribbles. Changing the pen from one hand to the other, Oliver then pushes the cap onto the pen and replaces it in the pot. He takes it out again and repeats the ritual. When he comes to replace the top he has difficulty because he has the wrong end. He tries and tries then stops and looks at it, puts it on the table and by accident picks it up the correct way and replaces the top and returns it to the holder. Oliver walks over to the books, selects a book and climbs onto the settee, opens it and looks at a page then looks at the adult and makes sounds, holding the book out to the adult. Looking at the pages he repeats this again and the adult sits on the settee and talks to Oliver about the pages. He gets up and walks towards the window sill, looks at bark and stones, touches them and then looks to the adult and continues his 'conversation'. She touches them and tells him what they are. He listens, looking from her face to the objects one by one. He then slides his hands over the bark and stones. He goes outside into the garden.

Oliver makes this trip two or three times a day, always to the drawing table first. He sometimes notices the painting easel in the wet room on his way out and stops and paints, or pokes his fingers in the playdough or stops at the washbasin and tries to turn the tap on. It might be argued that Oliver's experience in this instance is quite a lonely and solitary one.

Vygotsky (1978) emphasizes the sociocultural system within which children learn by participating in the activities of more skilled partners. He showed that children cooperating with adults or with children who are more capable in certain areas, can achieve more than on their own. While I accept this view and have confirmed it on many occasions in the nursery, in this instance it is my belief that Oliver was gaining a great deal from his solitary exploration of the world beyond the baby unit. The important issue is that he was not prevented from doing so by an adult who had a clear agenda in mind and who was hung up on safety issues and predetermined views of what it is appropriate for a 15-month-old to do.

I believe that when a child is absorbed completely in exploratory and creative activity it is sufficient for the adult to observe unobtrusively. All too often when an adult asks, 'What is it?', a child often looks blankly as if to say 'does it have to *be* something?' Very often a child will make up some response that will satisfy the adult and hopefully make them go away!

Very young children use creative activities as a non-verbal form of communication; they are of value to the young child while he/she is actively engaged in creative expression. Once finished they move off and into another activity. The doing or process is more important than the end product.

Adults have to be sufficiently observant, sensitive and perceptive to be able to know just when and where the fine division between experiences and expression of experiences comes and to be available to support children in their learning, not to impose themselves when children are coping well on their own. Debbie (3 years), when asked by a well-meaning, interested adult what she was going to paint, replied 'I don't know yet, I haven't started!'

Children do not need adults to *show* them how to draw or paint – they know, and they are so much better at it than the adults. Children's cats, houses and people are all very individual, all unique to them. Adults who are programmed on 'how to draw a cat' for a child, tend to draw identical cats, as they will houses and people – stereotyped and unimaginative. Children have a pure, unadulterated style, which they are confident in developing and expressing. Only when they have adults' examples, colouring-in books, confining lines and dots, do they begin to question their own creativity – striving to please and reproduce the adults' examples, only to strive in vain, becoming disillusioned and frustrated and then they begin to use words such as 'I can't'. Sensitive involvement of adults and shared learning experiences are to be encouraged as in the following examples.

On one occasion we went out in the garden and picked armfuls of daffodils. We buried our heads in the yellow – smelled, 'tasted', ran our fingers over petals, trumpets and the children were marching around, blowing trumpets and we all felt wonderful – just like the Wordsworth poem.

Francesca (3 years) mixed her yellow and green paint and painted an absolute 'profusion of yellow and green' – fresh, alive and spontaneous – then ran out to play.

Becky (5 years) was visiting us from school when her mum asked, 'Why don't you paint a picture?' Becky replied, 'I can't'. In the end her mother persuaded her to. She painted five straight green stalks and five yellow blobs at the top. What has happened to her confidence, esteem and creative expression between the ages of 2 and 5?

Children respond to an environment containing beautiful, interesting and curious things. It is our responsibility to ensure that they have the richest possible environment in terms of materials, equipment, appreciation, understanding and time with which to record and express their feelings and responses.

How does a child's creative experience affect later learning?

I believe that the child whose creative growth has been fostered develops:

- confidence in their own personal achievements;
- confidence to explore, experiment and believe that most things are possible;
- ongoing curiosity – which should be nurtured from the first months or even weeks;
- confidence in verbalizing their own thoughts and expressing ideas, opinions and the belief that these are of value;
- skills in close and careful observation, encouraged through interaction with adults, as seen in the examples of Lucy and Oliver in their very early months;
- a moral attitude and caring role towards the environment, each other and all living creatures (encouraged on a daily basis – through interaction with the environment, books, each other and sensitive adults).

I recently followed up the first children, who attended the nursery six years ago and came when they were 2 years of age. They are now 8. Their parents and teachers were asked to identify the qualities in the children which they could attribute to their experience in the nursery. The main areas in which the children 'stood out in mainstream school' were: confidence, self-esteem and an ongoing curiosity to question, wonder and verbalize. These are important attributes which, if developed early, equip children to respond positively to the demands they will face at subsequent stages in their educational lives.

Responding to SCAA for under-threes

The publication by the School Curriculum and Assessment Authority (1996) of *Desirable Outcomes for Children's Learning on Starting Compulsory Schooling* requires creative and imaginative thinking on the part of adults if the programme is to be implemented in ways that are relevant and meaningful for young children. Above all it is important that creativity and imagination are not stifled in an attempt to 'deliver' and 'tick off' what are, after all, natural, developmental milestones.

The following 'desirable outcomes' are included under the heading 'knowledge and understanding of the world':

They explore and recognise features of living things, objects and events in the natural and made world and look closely at similarities, differences, patterns and change. They talk about their observations, sometimes recording them and ask questions to gain information about why things happen and how things work . . . They explore and select materials and equipment and use skills such as cutting, joining, folding and building for a variety of purposes.

SCAA (1996: 4)

The close observations of children under 3 previously presented (together with the following case studies of very young children 'at work') show just how much of a foundation is being laid long before the child's first birthday, as they 'explore and recognise features of living things, objects and events in the natural and made world'.

The close observation of a spider illustrated in Figure 6.3, which he had found outside, shows just how skilfully Julian at 2 years, 10 months could reproduce what he had seen.

Under the heading 'physical development', SCAA (1996: 4) states:

Children move confidently and imaginatively with increasing control and co-ordination and an awareness of space and others. They use a range of small and large equipment and balancing and climbing apparatus, with increasing skill. They handle appropriate tools, objects, construction and malleable materials safely and with increasing control.

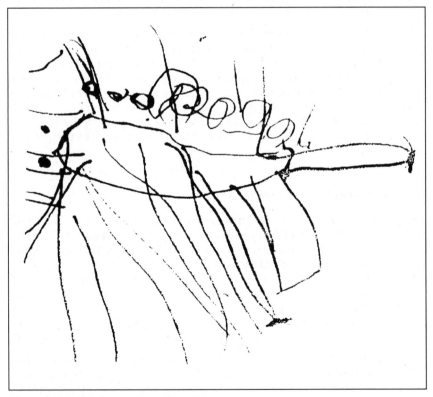

Figure 6.3 Julian's drawing of a spider

Under 'creative development', SCAA (1996: 4) says:

Children explore sound and colour, texture, shape, form and space in two and three dimensions. They respond in a variety of ways to what they see, hear, smell, touch and feel. Through art, music, dance, stories and imaginative play, they show an increasing ability to use their imagination, to listen and to observe. They use a widening range of materials, suitable tools, instruments and other resources to express ideas and to communicate their feelings.

I consider that all the issues highlighted in this chapter are relevant to the achievement of these 'desirable outcomes'.

I have given examples of children living life to the full, using a range of materials, increasing their aesthetic awareness and creative skill and ability. The important point is that they are doing all this in the company of adults who are knowledgeable and sensitive to the needs of very young children and who celebrate their achievements. These children are already achieving a great deal and they are not yet 3! I feel privileged that I am able to witness and celebrate their achievements.

References

Abbott, L., Ackers, J., Grant-Mullings, N., Griffin, B. and Marsh, C. (1996) *Educare for the Under Threes – Identifying Need and Opportunity*, Interim research report (July). Manchester: Esmée Fairbairn Charitable Trust/The Manchester Metropolitan University.

Bradley, R. H., Caldwell, B. M. and Elardo, R. (1979) Home environment and cognitive development in the first 2 years, *Developmental Psychology*, 15(3): 246–50.

Bronfenbrenner, U. (1968) Early deprivation in mammals and man, in G. Newton (ed.) *Early Experience and Behaviour*. Springfield, IL: Charles C. Thomas.

Department of Education and Science [DES] (1990) *Starting with Quality: Report of the Committee of Inquiry into the Quality of the Educational Experience offered to 3 and 4 year olds*. London: HMSO.

Goldschmied, E. (1987) *Infants at Work* (training video). London: National Children's Bureau..

Goldschmied, E. and Selleck, D. (1996) *Communication Between Babies in Their First Year*. London: National Children's Bureau Enterprises.

Goleman, D. (1996) *Emotional Intelligence: Why it Can Matter More than IQ*. London: Bloomsbury Publishing.

Lowenfeld, V. and Brittain, W. (1987) *Creative and Mental Growth*. London: Macmillan.

Nutbrown, C. (1994) *Threads of Thinking*. London: Paul Chapman Publishing.

Nutbrown, C. (ed.) (1996) *Children's Rights and Early Education*. London: Paul Chapman Publishing.

Piaget, J. (1951) *Play, Dreams and Imitation*. London: Routledge and Kegan Paul.

School Curriculum and Assessment Authority [SCAA] (1996) *Desirable Outcomes for Children's Learning on Starting Compulsory Schooling*. London: SCAA.

Vygotsky, L. (1978) *Mind in Society: The Development of Higher Level Psychological Processes*. Cambridge, MA: Harvard University Press.

7 | 'What's it all about?' – how introducing heuristic play has affected provision for the under-threes in one day nursery

Ruth Holland

Introduction

> Too many books and training materials bunch the needs of under fives together but we must take care to perceive the needs of each child as unique, and to acknowledge that they each have special learning needs at different stages in their development.
>
> (Rouse and Griffin 1992: 149)

The above statement describes a situation of which I have become increasingly aware. As co-owner/manager of a 60-place day nursery where over half the children are under 3, and approximately one third of children are under 2, part of my role is to oversee the planning of play and activities. Much of the material written about play is produced with 3- to 5-year-olds in mind, and does not specifically address the needs of younger children, with the result that play for children under 3 is often a watered down version of play aimed at 3- to 5-year-olds. For example a leaf printing activity may be carried out with a group of 3- to 5-year-olds with the aim of increasing the children's awareness of leaf shape or autumn colours and/or extending the children's painting skills, as well as many other possibilities. When this same activity is offered to a group of 18- to 24-month-old children who may be more interested in putting their hands in the paint, dripping paint from the brush or floating the leaves off the table, adults are often guilty of expecting the same response as they do from older children. We need to be careful that we are not guilty of fitting the child to the activity rather than the activity to the child.

One specific factor which should be considered when planning play provision for children under 3 is the tremendous rate at which development takes place. Two of the major milestones affecting children's play are mobility and speech acquisition; i.e. the needs of a small baby lying on a mat are going to be very different from the child who has just learned to walk, and again different to the child whose speech has become fluent.

Rouse and Griffin (1992: 154) point out, though, that development does not take place in neat uniform steps: 'such phases are not distinct, or an invariant sequence of play behaviour. They overlap and are part of a continuum of learning.'

An example I observed which illustrated this point was a 23-month-old child looking at a metal pan scourer (copper coloured). As Brittany picked the scourer up she looked at it in a puzzled manner, turned the scourer over several times, put it down, picked it up again, smelt it, passed it from hand to hand and eventually – having almost given up deciding what the object was – put it in her mouth to see if that gave her the answer. Brittany turned to using the methods she had used when younger to discover what an object was. Brittany's actions contradict developmental checklists which say that an 18-month-old child will no longer put toys in her mouth, for example (Sheridan 1973). While this developmental statement by Mary Sheridan would in general be true for Brittany, we have seen it is not always so. This, therefore, illustrates the need not to rely too heavily on developmental checklists when planning provision for a particular age group.

Heuristic play

In my quest to discover more about play for children under 3 I have found work around the concept of heuristic play particularly fruitful.

'Heuristic play' is a term used by the trainer and educator Elinor Goldschmied to describe the early stages of play in which children's absorption is predominantly for putting in and out, filling and emptying containers and receptacles of all kinds. Here there is no question of success or failure. It is all new discovery and there is no 'right' or 'wrong'. The child learns from observing directly what these objects will 'do' or 'not do', in sharp contrast to much of the 'educational' equipment which has a result predetermined by the design which has been devised by the adult maker.

Part of the adults' role is to collect, buy or make a good quantity of objects such as empty tins and metal jar caps, woollen pom-poms, wooden clothes pegs, wooden and metal curtain rings and ping pong balls. The underlying idea is that these objects should offer the widest variety of materials and that they should be available to the children in large quantities.

Hair curlers of differing diameter; large and small corks; rubber door stops; varied lengths of chain, fine- to medium-sized links, not large chains; and large bone buttons can also be added to the collection (Goldschmied 1987).

The role of the adult

The role of the adult is partly that of organizer in collecting, caring for and thinking up new types of interesting items. They unobtrusively reorder objects and initiate the collecting by the children and the putting away of the materials in bags. They are essentially a facilitator, and as such they remain quiet, attentive and observant. They may study a particular child and note down all that he or she does with the materials, recording the quality of the child's concentration. The children are fully aware of their presence, though they do not encourage or suggest, praise or direct what the children do. (Only if a child begins to throw things about and disturb the others is it a wise plan to offer a receptacle and encourage her to place the things into it.)

It is important for the adult, during this heuristic play period, to sit on a chair. In this way she can be available to all the children and watch carefully what is going on. When the children are active in a group adults are likely to miss a great deal of what is significant in their behaviour if they are not seated. A child left free to choose what she wants to do in this secure atmosphere will tell a sensitive observer a lot about herself and so increase our understanding of her as an individual.

Staff who have experienced conducting this kind of play session have noted that:

- an atmosphere of tranquil concentration develops;
- children become absorbed in pursuing their own exploration of the material for periods of half an hour and more, without direct reference to the adult;
- conflicts between the children are very infrequent because there are abundant materials, but at the same time there are many friendly interchanges between them, with gestures and early verbal comments;
- during the long nursery day this activity brings calm enjoyment both for them and for the adults. The staff have an opportunity to observe the children in a way which is not easy at other times in the busy day;
- where there are children under the age of 2 in a mixed age group, it is possible, when there is a staff member available, for her to give some special attention to a very small group. It offers a great advantage since often the younger children find they have to compete for attention with the older ones;
- as soon as a child begins to have some command of language the nature of her use of the material changes and items are put to an imaginative use as another, more complex, type of play emerges. Instead of 'What can I do with it?', the question moves to 'What can this object become?' For example, a wooden cylinder, instead of being popped through a hole, may be used as a feeding bottle for a doll. To link this to the treasure basket phase, the same cylinder has been used, by the seated baby, to grasp, suck and bang with.

Over the years Elinor Goldschmied has studied the development of young children under the age of 2 in many cultures and with different social backgrounds. I was, therefore, keen to watch the two videos she has produced: *Infants at Work* in which she introduces the treasure basket and *Heuristic Play with Objects*, which offer suggestions of play to meet the specific requirement of the under-twos. 'Heuristic' in this context means learning through exploration.

In the first video – aimed at babies who are sitting but not yet mobile – Goldschmied suggests the idea of the treasure basket, which is a shallow, sturdy basket full of a variety of everyday objects varying in weight, size texture, colour, smell, taste, temperature, etc. The babies can explore it using all their senses to discover *What the objects are.*

In the second video – aimed at children who are just mobile – Goldschmied suggests that materials be presented in a different manner, as the children now move on to see *What they can do with the objects.*

For this heuristic play the objects are provided in much larger numbers in order to prevent conflict between children who have not yet gained the concept of sharing. Containers are also provided so the objects may be placed in them, taken out, collected together, filled, emptied, sorted, shaken, rattled and a variety of other activities which appeal to the senses of curious babies.

Play and the under-twos

Some observations

Goldschmied (1987) recommends heuristic play for children 10 to 20 months old. As staff we made a conscientious decision to include this type of play in our curriculum. We decided that the most appropriate place to introduce this sort of play in our nursery was the Toybox room, where the children are 13 to 24 months old. One of my first observations involved two children, Richard and Harry (both 24 months), using the bobbins as trumpets, thus progressing along the continuum of learning from *What can they do with the objects?* to *What are they really for?* The use of the bobbins engaged the children's imagination and enabled them to make an attempt at deciding what the objects were really for, although at this stage it was quite clear that the former question was the more important.

I went on to compare this and other observations of this group with what has been written about play by Piaget, Smilansky, and Taklavar and Smith as described by Smith (1994: 16) and Hutt *et al.* (1989: 222). During my observations of heuristic play I did observe much of the sensory motor and exploratory play as described by Piaget, although I did not feel happy with the title 'practice play' he gave to the play of young infants aged 6 months to 2 years, as I feel it underestimates in some way the play experiences of this age group. The imaginative, pretend and sociodramatic play (which Piaget termed 'symbolic play') I only observed in the older children, such as Harry and Richard when they were playing trumpets, and Lucy (also 24 months) when she was using a length of chain as a necklace. Hutt *et al.* (1989) describe this relaxed, expressive and imaginative play as 'ludic' behaviour.

I believe that she has made an immense contribution to our view of play, moving us from the simplistic notion of 'it is what all young children do' to a recognition that it is a complex, high level activity which, like all learning, is developmental. She argues that under the umbrella term 'play' there are many different behaviours, and only through close observation of, and involvement in, young children's play can the adult really understand what is going on and begin to help children move on to the next stage. The terms 'ludic' and 'epistemic' play are used to distinguish two very different kinds of play behaviours; they require different responses from adults.

Epistemic play behaviour	*Ludic play behaviour*
• is concerned with acquisition of knowledge and skill problem solving	• is playful
	• is fun
• gathers information	• is lacking in specific focus
• is exploratory	• is highly mood dependent
• is productive	• has constraints which (when they exist) are imposed by the child
• discovers	
• is invention, task or work orientated	• does not need to involve adults
	• requires that adults should be sensitive to children's needs
• is relatively independently of mood state	• can be changed by insensitive intervention
• has constraints which stem from the nature of the focus of attention	• has the key features of enjoyment and fantasy
	• is unconstrained
• needs adults to:	• is idiosyncratic
– support	• is repetitive
– encourage	• is innovative
– answer questions	• is symbolic.
– supply information	
– be involved.	

Smilansky (1968) added a further category to Piaget's work, 'constructive play', in which objects are manipulated to construct or create something. I observed examples of such play during the session when Brittany (aged 23 months) stacked the bobbins, Lucy stacked the tins together, and Theo (13 months) placed the coat pegs all round the perimeter of the tin.

I did not observe any physical activity play, or rough and tumble play, as described by Taklavar and Smith. They wrote that this type of play fell into neither Piaget's or Smilansky's categories. What I did observe, though, was the epistemic behaviour as described by Hutt *et al.* (1989), which is play that is exploratory, intent, attentive and assimilatory. This has important implications for adult involvement or at least, adult availability, if (as Hutt argues) the presence of the adult in epistemic, as distinct from ludic play, is crucial.

Important issues

I was so impressed with the quantity and quality of epistemic behaviour, as described above, that I turned my thoughts to two questions: how can we extend the opportunities for these children to gain learning experiences through exploratory play? Does this pattern of mainly exploratory play with some constructive and some symbolic play repeat itself if different toys are provided?

Taking my first question, I know the answer cannot just be 'more heuristic play', as we have found that if this play is offered more than two or three times a week to each child they begin to lose interest. I believe that this could be overcome if we had access to limitless new materials to add and swap with the existing materials but, as we don't, then other answers need to be sought.

In an attempt to answer the question I set up a water play session following the guidelines for heuristic play. Other toys and possible distractions were removed as far as possible and there was enough equipment to avoid conflict over sharing. Staff took on the role of observers and did not intervene.

The resources for the activity comprised ten shallow trays set out on tables. Each tray contained either warm, cold, clear or coloured water, with either ice cubes, corks or stones. After a while tea strainers and small beakers were added.

As I observed this activity I found, as with the heuristic play, that the behaviour was predominantly epistemic.

Another instance was when I observed this same group of children taking part in a gluing activity. As with the previous two activities all other toys were removed, each child had their own paper, glue, spreader and cut pieces of tissue paper, and staff intervened as little as possible.

The epistemic behaviour was repeated. The object of the children's intent was the glue. A great deal of time was spent stirring, dipping, spreading and making marks, with the glue and spreader on the paper. Sticking the tissue paper on was mainly ignored, unless suggested by staff, and then very often it was done quickly so the child could get back to exploring the glue. The children spent an average of 30 minutes gluing – Louisa (aged 24 months) spent 40 minutes at this activity and would have continued for longer had it not been lunch time! This is a significant finding given that researchers involved in the Oxford pre-school project (Bruner 1980) showed surprise when 3-year-olds concentrated on an activity for five minutes.

These observations led me to believe that these activities had succeeded in beginning to answer my first question: the waterplay session and gluing sessions had indeed provided further opportunity for exploratory play. My next step was to have a brainstorming session with nursery staff to produce examples of other exploratory play ideas, as my observations made me think there is certainly a need to provide this age group with plentiful opportunities for this type of play. As Abbott (1994: 80) points out, 'Hutt showed clearly that exploration is a powerful forerunner to full-blown play. Many teachers and other educators are guilty of hurrying children on to "production" when the joy, excitement, and learning to be gained from exploring the materials comes first.'

To help answer my second question – does the type of play change if the toys are different? – I set up two activities, deliberately choosing equipment aimed at play which Hutt *et al.* (1989: 224–5) found to produce ludic behaviour. The first activity was an outdoor physical play session with bikes, cars and trucks, and the second session was one in which imaginative toys were provided, such as small cars and a road mat, dinosaurs, farm animals, zoo animals, and play people.

What I observed from the outdoor play was that during the first five to ten minutes, play was relaxed and the children were at ease as they pedalled the bikes and cars around. After that the children became less boisterous, and I observed children examining pedals, looking closely at wheels, poking twigs between spokes and generally becoming more intent. What had begun with a group of nine children aged 13 to 24 months, all displaying ludic behaviour, changed after five to ten minutes to individuals behaving in an epistemic manner.

This pattern repeated itself during the imaginative play session. Again, to begin with, there were lots of examples of imaginative play, with the cars being rolled along the floor with 'brum brum' noises and animals being walked along with 'clip clop' noises – but again after five to ten minutes children began to examine the toys, turning them over, feeling them, placing them, examining them, etc.

So, therefore, from my observations the answer to my second question is that different toys and equipment can affect whether 1-year-old children play in an epistemic or ludic manner, but not as much as might be expected. But a third question might be – what exactly should be the adult role in these different kinds of play behaviours?

Staff involvement

I feel that children of this age in our nursery already have well-developed epistemic behaviour, and that while staff have an important role in providing the materials, equipment, a suitable setting and a calm atmosphere for exploratory play, there is little need for intervention during such play – this could well disturb a child's concentration or opportunity to learn through doing something for him or herself. I feel an important role for staff during such play is that of observer, thus enabling the future needs of the individual children to be assessed. However, this is something I will continue to monitor since Hutt clearly points to the important role of adult availability to support children's epistemic play.

However, in contrast to Hutt I felt that the children's play which displayed ludic behaviour – the physical and imaginative play – could benefit much more from adult intervention, as the children demonstrated their ability to initiate ludic behaviour play but were unable to sustain it for very long, unlike older children, who I have observed playing imaginative games over several days without adult intervention. It must be remembered that Hutt's research was with 3- to 5-year-olds, and clearly there are differences between this age group and the under-threes in their ability to sustain ludic play.

In order to support children I believe staff need to become fully immersed in the play, so that they are a part of it. It may be that staff initiate games such as chase in the garden, or perhaps they look to extend existing play, for example, by becoming the car park attendant when the children are playing on the bikes and cars. There may be instances where the staff play together themselves in order to provide model examples, such as holding telephone conversations using toy telephones.

However, in whatever way staff become involved in children's play, it is useful to bear in mind the conditions needed to ensure good quality play as identified in the Rumbold Report (1990) and described by Abbott (1994: 85):

1 sensitive, knowledgeable and informed adult involvement and intervention;
2 careful planning and organization of the play setting in order to provide for and extend learning;
3 enough time for children to develop their play;
4 careful observation of children's activities to facilitate assessment and planning for progression and continuity.

I will discuss my own engagement with these four issues in turn.

With regard to the first issue, I have become aware of the need to share the new information and knowledge I have gained with staff, with the aim of improving the sensitivity of their involvement with children. This has mainly taken place through our normal weekly planning meetings and discussions with individual staff. A better way would be to have team meetings – but this is difficult to organize as they have to take place outside already long nursery hours. As a result we now have fewer whole-staff meetings, and these have been replaced with some team staff meetings.

The second issue of planning and organization has also been addressed through the revised meeting schedule. This has resulted in a definite change in the pattern of activity organization. Whereas previously one hour each morning and afternoon was allocated to 'planned activities' now this hour is scheduled for exploratory play, imaginative play or key worker activities. During activity sessions (ten in all during a week; five morning and five afternoon), exploratory play may take place for three sessions, imaginative play for two sessions and key worker activities for five sessions. The numbers are not fixed and staff choose the frequency to suit the children, and also vary the days to allow for part-time children to experience a variety of activities. (It should be noted that the day also includes free play, circle time and physical play both morning and afternoon.) To assist staff in their planning and organization it was decided to draw up brief guidelines for each type of activity (see Figure 7.1).

The third issue generally does not pose a problem for the under-twos as the 45-minute play sessions we operate do not appear to limit children's play. However, we do need to be aware that as children are developing, their concentration span will lengthen. For example Louisa, 24 months old, played for 40 minutes with the glue.

The fourth and final issue of observation and assessment is one which has developed not only as part of my own work with the under-twos, but also within the nursery as a whole.

Previously our observations and recording had been aimed at recording children's developmental success for sharing with parents at our twice yearly parents' evenings. These observations were continuous but not used in any structured way to plan future activities for the children.

---

1 *Exploratory play:* 30–45 minutes plus 15 minutes clearing-away time.
- Clear away all toys and remove as many distractions as possible.
- Create a calm, quiet atmosphere.
- Ensure there are enough materials, equipment and space so sharing is not necessary.
- Examples of materials which may be offered: wet sand, dry sand, water, ice cubes, large ice blocks, cooked spaghetti, jelly set in trays, playdough, clay, bread dough, twigs, leaves, fir cones, shells, glue, a variety of paints, unusual foods to taste, cornflour and water and a variety of everyday materials.
- Sit quietly and observe, offer reassuring smiles and nods but avoid talking or directing play.

2 *Imaginative play:* 30–45 minutes plus 15 minutes clearing-away time.
- Set the whole room up with role play equipment such as home corner, shop, telephones, dressing up, dolls, vehicles, or alternatively offer open-ended materials such as large boxes.
- Staff play homes/shopping, etc. in ways which will give example to children, lead the play or extend play initiated by children.

3 *Key worker activities:* 30–45 minutes plus 15 minutes clearing-away time.
- Plan these activities for children for whom you are the key worker.
- The activities chosen should be linked to the observations and evaluation made of each child.

Figure 7.1 Staff notes for activities in Toybox and Chatterbox room

The issue was raised with staff and they were in agreement that our present system needed to be reviewed. Staff felt they used observations in an informal manner to feed into planning activities but that this process could be improved.

Each member of staff is now responsible for observing every child for whom they are the key worker. The recording sheets are designed so each child has their own sheet. Observations are written on the left and evaluation and future planning on the right.

With staffing ratios being one adult to three children for children under 2, observation is not a problem although recording can be, owing to the physical demands of children of any age. For much of the day the staff literally 'have their hands full'.

When the frequency of observations was discussed three timescales were considered: monthly, weekly and daily. Monthly observations were immediately decided upon as being too infrequent as the development of children is far too rapid at this age.

Daily observations were considered and thought to be appropriate if we had the same group of children each day, but as we have a great number of part-time children, staff envisaged problems. Weekly observations were therefore chosen because not only did this allow for our part-time children, it fitted in with our present weekly planning of activities.

Play by 2- to 3-year-olds

Observations and findings

Having adopted nursery planning for the under-twos, our attention then focused on the 2- to 3-year-olds and the implications of planning for this age group. In order to gain further knowledge of the needs of the 2- to 3-year-olds in relation to exploratory and imaginative play, I undertook a series of observational exercises.

My first observation was of an exploratory play session involving the same children as 12 months earlier. Each child was provided with a tray of corn-flour and water, plus a variety of tools such as paintbrushes, spoons and glue spreaders. (The same guidelines for exploratory play as previously stated were followed.)

One of the first differences I noted was that a year later, these older children vocalized their thoughts, which they had not done earlier. As the children put their hands into the cornflour and water the following comments were made:

It's sticky.
It's cold.
It's cold and warm.
Where have my fingers gone?
It tickles.

It soon became apparent that space was also an issue with the older children. The trays had been placed on tables with the children sitting or standing alongside each other. When these children were younger they limited their play to their own tray and had little or no interaction with the other children. However, the older children were much more interactive. Theo painted his hands with the cornflour and water; Harry copied. Harry then dripped cornflour into Theo's tray and, later, both Harry and Theo placed the utensils in each other's trays and pretended they were boats.

I was unsure as to whether the reasons for these changes were purely developmental or if the amount of space each child had to play in affected how the children played. I therefore set up a second exploratory play session with glue, identical to the session 12 months earlier, except that now each child was given their own table.

I observed there was still some interaction between the children although it was a lot less than in the previous activity:

• As Patrick spoke of snakes, Ryan joined in and they held a short conversation.

- A few minutes later Patrick and Ryan spoke about bats. Guy joined in the conversation. Also towards the end of the session Patrick and Ryan started to pretend the collage materials were objects.

However, the majority of the play was epistemic:

- Ryan carefully covered all of his paper with glue, taking care to go into the corners.
- Patrick dribbled his glue and talked of snakes.
- Jolyon having stuck some collage material onto his paper, carefully dripped glue around each piece of collage.

Another difference from 12 months previously was that all the children except one added collage material to the paper and glue. There were many examples of epistemic behaviour as each child applied the materials in different ways:

- Jo chose all red pieces of material.
- Guy chose all shiny pieces of material.
- Patrick matched collage materials together on the paper.

The one child who did not add collage material treated the glue as if it were paint and made comments such as 'I'm doing daddy.' She also painted her hands with the glue. As this child was new to nursery, I suspected that she may have not experienced glue in this manner before but had painted previously, and may have been using the known to make sense of the unknown.

Following this session, I discussed my observations with the staff present and working with this group of children.

We all agreed that the children had played mainly in an epistemic manner but we were aware that there were two factors which had become more important when providing 2- to 3-year-olds with exploratory play rather than when they were under 2. These were:

- the need for a quiet, calm atmosphere in the room. We found that if an adult spoke during the activity in a normal level of voice then the children started to talk, but if staff only spoke when essential and then in a whisper the children carried on playing intently.
- the need for each child to have sufficient space to explore the materials uninterrupted. My initial views were that when the children played together then their behaviour tended to change from epistemic to ludic – although I would need to do some follow-up observations to be sure of this.

Having noted the requirements for successful exploratory play we went on to discuss the frequency with which this type of play might be offered to the children. We felt that exploratory play should be offered at least once a week, with the frequency increasing for the group children nearer 2 than 3.

My next observations were of the children playing in the home corner. In addition to the home corner itself, the room had been set out with dolls, dolls' clothes, cots, etc., shopping trolley, shopping basket, till, etc. children's mattresses, shopping bags and dressing-up clothes.

During this session I noted a wider variation in how the children played than in previous sessions.

John and Alex (each 26 months) were new to the group, having just moved from the under-twos group. They both chose to stay near an adult. John was keen to talk to the adult and constantly asked questions or made statements, such as 'What are you doing, Ruth?'

John initiated short bursts of imaginative play. For example, he picked up the iron and announced 'Here is the iron', and proceeded to iron some dolls' clothes for about two minutes and then moved off.

Alex sat very quietly observing the group. Alex did not initiate any play but when I initiated a game of peepo where he pretended to switch the toy TV on and off, he laughed and carried on the game for over five minutes.

Guy and Ryan, who are now nearly 3, played quite differently. They played together all the time, although their focus for play changed constantly. During the 45 minutes, they played with the pizzas in the home corner, moved to dressing up, took the trays out of the dishwasher and announced they were rabbit cages, went to bed, etc.

I felt their imaginative play had developed in that they were much more confident and prolific at initiating imaginative play. With careful planning and sensitive intervention, staff could help them to develop their imaginative play even further.

The final two in the group were very different again. Meg and Jo played constantly with the dolls for the full 45 minutes. Jo (33 months) was very involved with the dolls and only spoke if she wanted help with fastening the dolls' clothes, etc. Meg (29 months) often copied Jo and would want whatever Jo had so she could be the same. A member of staff sitting next to Jo and Meg intervened when Meg showed signs of frustration at not being able to sit the doll up or if she was unable to find the same toys as Jo had.

On discussion with staff after this session, we noted the following points:

1 As children's imaginative play is based on life experience, it is important to be aware of these young children's relative inexperience, and to match the props for imaginative play accordingly.
2 There is a wide variation in the ability of children aged 2 to 3 to play imaginatively, and observation by staff followed by careful planning and sensitive intervention is required.
3 As the younger children appear to learn by watching older children's behaviour, it may be that imaginative play sessions with a wider age range may be beneficial for the younger children.
4 Staff may also 'play' and act as role models with the under-twos.
5 The frequency of imaginative play (as opposed to exploratory play) should increase as the children's imaginative play develops over the year between the ages of 2 and 3.

The result has been that currently in our nursery the children aged 2 to 3 are offered five to six key worker activity sessions, one to two exploratory play sessions and two to three imaginative play sessions, at the discretion of the staff.

In conclusion

Imaginative, exploratory and key workers' activities are now an established part of our nursery life for children under 3.

Of these activities it is the exploratory play sessions, I feel, that represent the biggest change. This would probably be the same for most pre-school establishments, as Hutt *et al.* (1989: 226) point out: 'Pre-school environments are structured in such a way as to encourage primarily ludic rather than epistemic activity . . . Free play, or ludic activity, clearly has an important effect on psychological development, but it requires appropriate counter-balancing by epistemic behaviour.'

I feel the quiet atmosphere and attentive behaviour of the children in exploratory play sessions can be likened to the behaviour of children when being taught in a whole-class situation – an idea to which I previously would have been averse.

However, my observations have led me to believe that the quiet atmosphere of these sessions and the attentive behaviour of the children provides them with excellent opportunities for learning.

The future

We are currently considering the implications of the *Desirable Outcomes for Children's Learning* (SCAA 1996) for the children in nursery. Although the learning outcomes are aimed at 4-year-olds, we will need to be aware of any ways in which they may affect the provision for the younger children, and the lessons learned in studying the under-threes which may help the older children achieve these learning outcomes.

However, we believe that the way we are currently resourcing and managing play in the nursery provides a firm foundation for learning and will, therefore, lead to desirable outcomes – whoever is monitoring them!

References

Abbott, L. (1994) 'Play is ace!': developing play in schools and classrooms, in J. Moyles (ed.) *The Excellence of Play*. Buckingham: Open University Press.

Bruner, J. (1980) *Under Five in Britain*. Oxford: Grant MacIntyre.

Goldschmied, E. (1987) *Infants at Work* (training video). London: National Children's Bureau.

Goldschmied, E. and Hughes, A. (1992) *Heuristic Play with Objects* (video). London: National Children's Bureau.

Hutt, J., Tyler, S., Hutt, C. and Cristopherson, H. (1989) *Play, Exploration and Learning*. London: Routledge.

Rouse, D. and Griffin, S. (1992) Quality for the under threes, in G. Pugh (ed.) *Contemporary Issues in the Early Years*. London: Paul Chapman Publishing/National Children's Bureau.

Sheridan, M. (1973) *Children's Developmental Progress from Birth to Five Years.* Windsor: NFER

Smilansky, S. (1968) *The Effects of Sociodramatic Play on Disadvantaged Preschool Children.* New York: Wiley.

Smith, P. (1994) Play and the uses of play, in J. Moyles (ed.) *The Excellence of Play.* Buckingham: Open University Press.

8 | 'You really understand what I'm saying, don't you?' – partnership with parents of children with special needs

Brenda Kyle

The background

As a teacher working in a fairly traditional establishment, I had heard the term 'Opportunity Group' and, though I understood what it meant, I little knew how important this concept was to become to me. I taught in the infant department of a weekly boarding school for children with special educational needs, working in comparative isolation from the children's parents. The few opportunities I had to talk with parents made me realize over and over again how families with a child with a disability were struggling. I saw how disability affects the whole family: parents, siblings, grandparents and so on. No matter how effective the programme was for the child in school, if parents had already got into a pattern of failure and despair, they were in for a fairly rough time when they resumed care for their child at weekends and holidays. I recognized that most of the families whose children started school at the age of 4+ had struggled through those preceding years, with little help. True, in most cases, the child had received input from various sources: peripatetic teaching, nursery or playgroup sessions, medical input, paramedical input, etc., but nobody had been there for the parents and siblings. Parents looked forward to the commencement of school as the solution to all their difficulties, only to find that it was no solution at all. Their own problems still had not been addressed. My appointment to head a nursery – which had a policy of integrating children with special educational needs (including *all* disabilities) and which also incorporated an Opportunity Group – opened up the whole new area of family work that I had instinctively felt was so neglected. Traditionally teachers were not comfortable with too many parents around. I quite clearly remember discussing the post I was to take up with a teaching colleague, who said 'The first thing you want to do is get rid of all those parents!'

What is an Opportunity Group?

The basic idea of an Opportunity Group is to provide an environment where parents/carers can come with their pre-school children. Here they will have access to a wide range of toys and equipment and also to a multidisciplinary staff. This is a concept so simple that it almost sounds too easy, and it may be that very fact that has caused it to be seen as an unimportant resource in the minds of some professionals. The philosophy of integration was unusual when this particular nursery started almost four decades ago, but that should no longer be an issue anywhere. All parents/carers are welcome with their children. Some come because they have heard that we are a good nursery, we are well equipped, it is a lovely building and all the facilities are 'user friendly'. They want their child to have the best possible start in life and they would like to be involved. Families with children with disabilities or special needs may have been referred by a health visitor, paediatrician, social worker or GP; they may simply have heard about us some other way. The building is bright, inviting and, above all, non-threatening. A whole range of play equipment for indoors and outdoors is available. The staff includes mainstream and special education teachers, a play specialist, a physiotherapist, a speech and language therapist and nursery nurses, all of whom are ready to talk with parents. They advise, support, encourage and communicate the importance of play and how children learn through play. All are welcomed as part of a large, happy family. The emphasis is on encouraging parents to see themselves as the experts on their children, to see their children as individuals of value and worth and not simply as a child with a label, for example a Down's Syndrome child or a cerebral-palsied child. It is this last fact that parents really respond to with enthusiasm.

A typical referral to the Opportunity Group

The routine telephone call from a local health visitor was typical of many I received requesting that I see a family with a 2 1/2-year-old. I have grown to know this health visitor well and respect her. I knew the anxiety in her voice meant a real concern for her clients which she felt she could share with me. She briefly outlined the background, and I made an appointment for her to come along with the family. I recognized immediately all the submerged anxieties as the parents with their little girl nervously introduced themselves. As frequently happens, mum did most of the talking with dad interjecting the occasional pertinent comment. She explained that they had accepted a place at a local playgroup with some relief, hoping that there the child would 'run off' some of the never-ending supply of the energy she had which left mum drained at the end of the day. But quite soon after starting mum had begun to dread picking-up time, as there always seemed to be a negative comment about her behaviour. Finally they had been asked to keep her at home because she was a 'naughty little girl' who never listened and who pushed the other children. By this stage of the story mum was tearful so I gently asked her to tell me about what happened at home: how the little girl played, what they enjoyed doing together, whether they looked at books, did she seem to understand instructions, did she use language? Mum confessed that she was very lively, embarrassingly so in public places, that she could not seem to concentrate on any one thing for long and that she was baffled as to how to play with her because she did not seem able to play. She was also worried about her lack of language but she hastily explained there was a family history of children being 'slow to talk'. She felt that she should be able to cope with her daughter without needing help. By the time the health visitor had picked up on her anxieties she was in despair with her own failure and the thought that people perceived her child as naughty. I explained a little about my own perception of the situation. I felt that, perhaps among other things, her daughter was not understanding the messages given to her. I outlined how we would work with them as a family in the Opportunity Group, and her relief was visible. With a smile that transformed her face, she said 'You really understand what I'm saying, don't you!'

How does it work?

First impressions

One of the most important principles is that families feel welcome – but a comment made by the head of a local school made me evaluate what exactly it is that we do offer. He asked, 'How do you get parents to stay?' It had never occurred to me that parents would not want to stay; in fact the comment took me aback. He went on to explain that in his experience parents usually wanted to leave their children and were only too happy to hand over the responsibility. So initially the welcome is of utmost importance. There is a big difference between coming because a child is disabled, and coming because it is a good playgroup and a pleasant place to be. It takes a lot of courage to put a foot over the doorstep and introduce yourself and your needs. Therefore that first greeting must be warm and positive; at that time parents must be helped to feel that all you are interested in is them and their child.

We are fortunate in having a secretary with a gift for just that. She is the first person parents/carers see as they step through the door into the foyer. Her ability to convey all that we stand for in her welcome is one of our precious assets and, as she introduces them to me or to one of the other key members of staff, you sense already that they feel they have got over the first hurdle. Sometimes we know nothing about the family; with others we have had a brief résumé from whoever has made the referral. With some children the disability will be obvious – the child may have Down's Syndrome or cerebral palsy – but with some children it is not so obvious. After the initial introductions I usually invite the parents to tell me a little about their child. In this way almost all the information I need is forthcoming without me having to ask questions. If it does not come, it will keep! There is no need to pry into painful areas; parents have a right to their own privacy and this is respected. Why should they bare their soul to someone they hardly know? The briefest of details are taken down at this stage. Families are shown round the nursery and given the chance to observe the different groups interacting and also to make their own comments and ask questions. Key members of staff are introduced on the way round, with a brief explanation of their role; families are then introduced to a few other parents/carers. These are usually mothers, but not always. Fathers are welcome and come when they can; some children may be with a carer. The family is then left to talk with one member of staff, thereby easing them over the awkward feelings of unfamiliarity with surroundings and routine. To the untrained eye our involvement at this stage could appear understated, but we feel it is most important that parents are not bombarded with questions and facts on their first visit. We have found, and feedback confirms, that parents appreciate the relaxed way in which they are allowed to become part of an established group. We have also found this approach helps to dissipate all their pent up fears and distress; we gently accept all that may come bubbling to the surface and spill out as they find, with relief, that there is someone to listen.

Quite recently a family arrived unexpectedly, led by a mother carrying an engaging 18-month-old little girl with Down's Syndrome. Grandmother accompanied them with baby brother, 5 weeks old in a portable car seat. Tagging along, looking uncomfortable and unsure, was the mother's adult sister, who had obvious special needs. Although, on the surface of things, it seemed that the family had sought out the nursery for their little girl, wanting to give her the opportunity of integration and wanting to be actively involved in those vital early developmental stages, there was also within that family group a whole hidden agenda to be addressed. The very lively little girl had needed heart surgery in the early months and her parents, in addition to adjusting to the fact that she had Down's Syndrome, also had the anxiety of her facing major surgery. Their new baby had a reflux problem and they had to cope with the trauma of projectile vomiting, weight loss, lack of sleep and colic. Grandmother had tried to help. She was distressed for her daughter and her grandchildren; she also had the memories of her own experiences in the past – still very much with her – memories of bringing up her other daughter with special needs. This complicated family situation needed sensitive support as they slowly unravelled the story. Probably the most helpful thing we did for them on that first afternoon was to take mum and grandmother into a quiet room for a cup of tea, while staff played with the children and someone talked to the sister.

The Opportunity Group environment

Visitors to the nursery often comment on the atmosphere of the nursery. It is situated on two floors. The nursery school takes place each morning for children aged between 2 years 9 months and 5 years. This is a 50-place nursery with a ratio of 35 mainstream children to 15 children with special needs. In the afternoons the nursery school operates upstairs only for 25 children, allowing the Opportunity Group to be held downstairs for the 0- to 3-year-olds. As people look around they observe a bright, exciting environment with little groups of parents, children and staff engaged in activities and conversation with and alongside each other. The centre of the nursery is taken up with two soft play rings positioned on a soft rug. Placed around these are a variety of toys, baby chairs, activity centres and mirror cubes. There is a sunken sand pit, the envy of many nursery schools, which children can get into. There are table toys, jigsaw areas, a book corner, water play, dough, an imaginative play area, a soft play room with trampoline and a ball pool. A tactile experience is planned daily, and outdoor play is available. Parents and children are encouraged to try all the areas. We also have a light sensory room, which can be either soothing or stimulating, depending on the equipment in operation. A projector or spot light helps to identify just what children with a visual impairment are able to focus on and gives a starting point from which to introduce other materials: bubble tube, fibre optics, shiny paper which reflects light, and so on. If children are distressed, the room has a wonderful calming effect; there are few children who do not respond to the changing images of an undersea scene. They look in wonder as a giant octopus floats round the room followed by a deep sea diver and a whale. Parents very quickly appreciate the benefits too.

Interactions

Parents are taken by surprise by the normality of the organization. They have been told by professionals or others that the people in this nursery are experts and specialists. They come with their child not quite knowing what to expect but with some vague notion or hope that we will put things right. I sometimes feel that our reputation is far greater than the work we do! They want their child 'therapied' – speech and language, physiotherapy, some special educational input, a structured programme – so that they can feel that 'someone is doing something' and maybe that 'something will make everything all right'. As we get to know the families we gently explain our philosophy and that, although we cannot wave a magic wand, nor do we have a miracle cure, there are many, many ways in which we can help, support and heal some of the hurts. We cannot make great promises for the future but we can make it easier for the family to cope from day to day, helping to make the child's quality of life as rich as possible and to give every opportunity for development.

What we do emphasize is the importance of the role of the parents/carers in the development of their children: how to encourage a response with the most basic pieces of equipment, for example a feely bag; how to encourage language development, how ordinary activities throughout the day can be an extension of the physiotherapy programme; in fact, how they can be in control if only they are given support, advice and encouragement. They are the most important people in the lives of their children and they need the confidence to acknowledge that.

The parents I referred to earlier, who came so nervously with their little girl, needed first of all to begin to regain some self-confidence and also to regain their joy in their child. The information that others perceived her as naughty, their struggles to cope with her, and that odd feeling growing stronger every day that she certainly did not appear to play like other children, all combined to create an overwhelming feeling of despair. They needed to be helped to see their little girl again as a little girl and not merely as a problem. Mum said that she did not play at home, she threw everything; if she did play with toys she would not play on her own, she wanted mum all the time, she would not allow mum to get on with anything.

Through observation of the interaction between the child and her mother we were able to help mum to see (and this took many weeks) that perhaps the little girl had been surrounded by too many toys that she was not quite ready for. In fact, this little girl was still at quite an early stage of play and exploration and too many demands were being made of her. Emptying and filling cupboards, baskets and boxes, we explained, is a vital stage of development. It can be made fun and should be encouraged in as many ways as possible. Neither will small children of this age 'go away and play'. It is important that mum is there to encourage, take part, extend and expand on play opportunities and language. Language input for this little one had to be simplified and had to be focused. She had switched off from too many confusing messages that she simply did not understand. Progress was slow, and to say we put everything right in a matter of weeks would be an oversimplification. We needed to, and still need to, give lots of support. The little girl transferred to the nursery after a term in the Opportunity Group, where she continues to make good progress but still has considerable language difficulties.

In the Opportunity Group parents and children are encouraged to take part in the activities right from the beginning. If their child is just a baby or is an older child who is not walking, then they join the activities in the centre of the floor. If their child is walking then they can move from area to area as they wish. The staff move among the little groups, talking to parents, encouraging play, offering advice or assistance as needed. Some parents wish to see the physiotherapist or the speech and language therapist and they may go off to a quieter area for consultation, but often they are seen working together on the nursery floor. A nursery assistant organizes an art activity in which parents and children participate together. This is the very beginning of sitting down and concentrating on a teacher-directed activity, and is a good model for parents who are often nonplussed as to know what to do with their children at home as they develop.

At a given time in the afternoon all the toys are tidied away and we have a singing time together. The children sit on their carer's knee and enjoy running through a repertoire of well-known nursery rhymes, action songs and finger rhymes. These are almost always in the same order every day because children love to anticipate what is coming next. It is surprising how many of today's young parents are reluctant to sing to their children, but in an already established group they take their place with everyone else. Perhaps they are a little self-conscious initially but they very soon forget themselves as they see the obvious enjoyment on their children's faces. All children respond to rhythm and music; in some instances this may be the very first activity mother and child have shared with mutual enjoyment. The opportunity for eye and body contact is invaluable. The bonus is that once this music is established at the nursery it will be carried on at home.

After the singing session comes the taste experience. Children sit in family groups with one adult at the table. The object is to widen children's experiences of textures and flavours of food. Children are frequently poor eaters, at the least picky, at the worst food-refusers; it astonishes parents that they will attempt food at the nursery they would not even look at when at home. The different foods we provide each week give mothers ideas as to what to try at home. The family grouping at the table is also important. The children are expected to sit down to eat and drink: in some families that is unheard of.

That is actually where the afternoon ends. Nothing extraordinary seems to have happened. It has been busy, even noisy; to the untrained eye it could appear a little chaotic. So why is it so successful, why do we have a waiting list of approximately 100 under-threes whose parents want to be part of what we have to offer? (Children with special needs are admitted straight away, they do not have to wait.) Perhaps we should look at some of the work more closely and begin to unravel the whole.

Special needs

Beginnings

Parents who give birth to children with special needs share common feelings. If it is obvious that the child has special needs at birth the exhilaration of a newborn baby is very soon diluted by a whole range of emotions. Disbelief, a feeling of dreaming, hoping that it is a dream, is replaced by flat reality; anger, despair, isolation, guilt, failure, depression and even denial, come in turn and flood the senses. All parents have spoken of these feelings. Disability feels very isolating. The world is geared for what is normal; it goes on as usual all around and the family is left in a little cocoon of special needs where none of the normal rules seem to apply. Even in the hospital ward the route starts to be different, and parents feel unable to join in the normal post-natal plans others families are engaged in. Instead they are the recipients of sympathetic glances and hushed whispers in their direction. Sometimes they are even avoided because of the embarrassment of others. Thankfully maternity units handle disability with much more skill and sensitivity than in the past, but there are still instances of insensitive blunders. It is an acknowledged fact that the bearer of bad news is often the focus for the anger of the receiver; no matter how well the situation has been dealt with, parents often feel medical staff are responsible for their hurt and pain. Consequently, they are not the people parents turn to for advice and support.

Children who are diagnosed from birth can come to us very early, as young as a few months old. Parents are coping in the best way they can and reacting in different ways: some are dazed and bewildered, some are defensive and protective, some angry and hurt. We must be ready to absorb and gently, very gently, attempt to meet their needs. In most instances, with such very young children it is a simple matter of having the time to listen. Hours are spent in allowing the parents to unload, to talk through how they feel, not giving answers (because we do not have them), simply just listening. I have used the term 'parents' because we welcome fathers, but it is usually mothers. Fathers may come on the initial visit but generally they must get on with their necessary task of resuming work and earning a living. This factor can lead to resentment within the family, with mothers feeling that father leaves the home and his problems behind in the morning, gets on with his separate life and then picks it up in the evening. Mothers will say that dad is more detached, less involved, does not see the problems as she does. And this is sometimes the case, for mothers are by their very presence, day in and day out, emotionally entangled and cannot take the more objective view that their partners can. The Opportunity Group acts as a safety valve for mothers. They feel that they can share things here that they cannot even admit to their partners. Often, as well as tears, much laughter is heard as they relax with staff and with each other.

There are parents who have spent the first few weeks or months with their children completely oblivious to the heartache ahead because their children's disability has not become apparent. In many ways this group of people has an even more difficult time, feeling that the child they cherished has been taken away from them. Often parents have spent months struggling with the knowledge that something is wrong. These parents experience emotional torture, from their first niggling suspicions when they begin to compare with their friend's children as developmental milestones are not reached, through to doctor's and hospital appointments. When finally somebody comes up with a diagnosis, their problems are exacerbated by the feeling that nobody understands and nobody seems to be doing anything. Parents of children with language and social communication disorders have a particularly difficult time. Parents are convinced that in the beginning the child was perfectly normal and that language had begun to develop. Some have home videos to prove that the child was making progress, had eye contact, babbled and was beginning to use single words and even phrases, but then things began to go wrong. The parents are desperate for help and cannot understand why intensive speech therapy will not simply put everything right. Working with all these parents demands understanding and skill from a team experienced, not only in the development of children with special needs, but who also have the ability to communicate confidence to the carers, assuring them that they will one day resume control. As families share they help each other because talking through a problem is helpful, not only in getting someone else's perspective, but in enabling themselves to see it more clearly.

Reactions

Many hopes and aspirations go through the minds of parents as they anticipate the birth of their child. None of these plans presume that their child may have learning difficulties or physical disabilities. The adjustment needed is of giant proportions and can only be made in tiny steps forward. The phrase, so often used, of parents not yet having 'come to terms' with their child's disability, is too easily said.

I believe parents make adjustments, sometimes major, sometimes minor, but they slowly edge forward with the right help and support to being able to cope. Occasionally, and this initially takes them by surprise, they take steps backward. It is important to warn them that this may happen, sometimes at critical stages of development, but sometimes for no obvious reason at all.

Reaction to disability varies enormously: some see it as a tragedy, others as a challenge. To yet others it is a fact about their child that brings a simple acceptance and a determination to integrate the child fully into the family. Many parents will tell you, as the child gets older, that their lives have been enriched because of their experiences. This is sometimes a difficult concept for new parents to understand. Here the support group which forms naturally with the Opportunity Group is very important. Parents gently encourage one another as they share thoughts they are not always so ready to share with those who have no concept of what it is like to have a child with a disability. Questions asked vary. Some cannot possibly be answered – 'Why me?' 'Why didn't "they" pick this up in pregnancy?' This is not the time for answers but a time to listen and let the hurt and anger out. Other parents come to talk to us who are not even sure they want to take their baby home from hospital: they come for advice, to look at how other parents are coping and what the children are like as they begin to sit up and take notice and be noticed. They pose questions such as: 'Is it fair to give this child our home; maybe he would be better adopted by somebody who really chose to have him?' 'How will it affect our lifestyle?' 'What about the other children?' Somehow it seems safe to test these thoughts and, although we would not feel in a position to persuade parents either way, we give space to think aloud. If parents do decide to take the child home they need to know that those working with them understand their feelings and are not judging them.

Because of the non-statutory nature of our provision some parents feel safer with us. It is sometimes the case that a parent has a 'niggle' about their child that they hardly dare voice to anyone, often initially not even to us. But by sensitive questions and observation it becomes apparent that the mother does have anxieties, sometimes real, sometimes imagined. In the Opportunity Group they do not feel that they are 'in the system'. Parents worry that matters will be taken out of their hands, and the professionals will take over and make decisions about their child in which they have no part. As one mother put it, 'She will end up on somebody's list, somewhere, and I will not know about it?' We can reassure them and tell them that if there is a need for further investigations, we will be with them at every stage and nothing will happen without their prior knowledge and consent.

Our role

I stress again that it takes skilled staff to meet the variety of needs that crop up daily: staff who are well experienced in the stages of child development, who understand how children learn and who have the confidence and the patience to wait for those tiny steps of movement. They must also be able to transmit a confident, positive attitude to parents. Often children have 'failed' somewhere before parents bring them to us, a fact that hurts parents deeply. We see little point in going through a checklist to fail them again. With that in mind we do not make any formal assessments until the child is about 2 1/2 years old. The activities we are looking for children to achieve are the kind that parents can easily understand and share with their children. We keep a list to which parents have access. It starts at a very basic level and moves through to more complicated tasks. Although it is developmental, it is not age related, and parents can easily pick out things to do with their children in the nursery and at home. It includes such things as:

1 Will hold something put in hand for one to two seconds.
2 Hands open some of the time; plays with fingers.
3 Stops crying when talked to.
   Shakes rattle.
4 Enjoys boisterous play.
   Puts out hand to object.
5 Likes looking at self in mirror.
6 Deliberately drops toys.
   Cooperates at hidey-boo.
7 Throws.
   Bangs toys together.
8 Puts two toys together (rattles spoon in cup).
9 Takes lid off a box.
   Looks at books with adult.
10 Copies three-brick tower.
   Combs hair – mum – doll – self – sequenced play.
11 Turns two/three pages of book.
12 Takes off shoes, socks, hat.
13 Pours water/sand from one container to another.
14 Will listen to a short story.
15 Good pincer grip.
16 Builds six/seven-brick tower.
   Situational play (doctor, postman).
17 Doll play.
18 Will copy train of four bricks.
19 Screws and unscrews.
   Runs and climbs.
20 Can stick two bricks together – Duplo, Stickle-bricks.
21 Snips paper with scissors.

Parents find it helpful to have the importance of play explained to them, how children learn through exploratory play, mouthing, filling, emptying, etc., to see how language emerges and how vital their role is. It is encouraging to see parents' confidence grow as play takes on a whole new meaning and they realize, with a greater understanding, what their child will achieve.

When the time does come for more formal assessment at the age of $2^1/_2$, parents and children know us fairly well. The special education teacher, the physiotherapist and the speech and language therapist are familiar figures with whom they feel quite comfortable. For many years we have used the PIP Developmental Charts (Jeffree and McConkey 1976). We talk to parents about the charts, encourage them to take them home, observe their child, fill them in and bring them back for further discussion. This way parents feel part of the assessment programme, and it is positive in that it builds on what children have already achieved. Often parents can only see what the child cannot do; this chart helps them to see the stages involved before a major milestone is reached. It also gives the staff a good baseline for when the child starts in the nursery. We hold termly meetings with the staff from the Child Development Unit attached to the local hospital; parents can feel confident that we are all working together for the best results for whole family.

Integration

Most of this chapter has focused on children with special needs, but all our families are equally important and all gain from the experience of integration. Most young mums look forward to the birth of their child with happy anticipation, planning the future in the belief that everything will be perfect. But babies have not read the textbooks and things do not always go according to plan. Years ago, grandparents or other experienced members of the family were around to advise, but the extended family, in many instances, has disappeared. Young parents can feel very isolated and, at times, overwhelmed by the job of parenthood. They welcome the chance to meet up with other families and learn about play development. They also need reassurance that they are doing a good job, that it does not really matter if their child does not conform to a preconceived pattern; the most important thing is to enjoy each other and those early years which pass so quickly, and to make the most of the opportunities.

We seem to achieve success in this area: visitors to the nursery comment on the happy 'buzz' as children and parents make the water wheel spin, put spoonfuls of flour into the tiny lorries and dumper trucks, experiment with the playdough, build sandcastles or are involved in any of the many other activities set out for them in the nursery.

However, even with this group, there can be real anxieties and it is a relief to have someone to talk these through with. Among our families there will be single parents, families where the main earner has been made redundant, those anxious about their own health, those with post-natal depression or illnesses. These people all need to know that we are available for them and have time to listen, advise and support. The number of grandparents looking after grandchildren is growing. This group, although well experienced at looking after children, often feel unsure of themselves. They are aware of changing times and practices and sometimes lack confidence, certainly lack stamina, and they are without a network of friends having young children. They can feel very isolated, and at a loss as to how to cope with very small children for a full day, five days a week. They are particularly appreciative of the support from the staff and the opportunity to mix with young mums and their children.

The toy library

The toy library is a valuable resource. This 'Aladdin's Cave' for children is packed full of toys and equipment to suit all levels of development from birth to 12. The toy library organizer is infectiously enthusiastic about this project and is always on hand to make helpful suggestions as to what exactly would be the best thing to take home for a child with visual impairment or poor coordination or, even – and this is by no means the least important aspect – what would simply be fun. The range of toys varies from simple 'feely bags' through to toys operated by touch switches and sound. She is nothing if not practical and can frequently be heard suggesting to parents too eager to move onto 'scientific toys' that they get out their pans and bowls and wooden spoons and allow their offspring to experiment with sound, cause and effect, emptying and filling.

Summary

If I had attempted to condense this chapter into a few lines, I would say 'an Opportunity Group is a place where families are accepted and encouraged, where the importance of play is demonstrated, where children and parents are given time to develop at their own pace, where families have access to professionals, where people can "test" their own thoughts and feelings, where parents are important people and where all children are valued.' Is that unrealistic?

It is not easy to convey through words the creatively happy atmosphere of parents and children engaged in learning together through play, but we believe it to be of utmost importance. The remark of a distressed mother of a severely physically handicapped little boy remains clearly in my mind. She was relating how an insensitive professional had said that she seemed to have little experience in mothering her handicapped child. In exasperation she said, 'Where are we supposed to get this experience, for heaven's sake?'

Reference

Jeffree, D. M. and McConkey, R. (1976) *PIP Developmental Charts* (Hester Adrian Research Centre, University of Manchester). London: Hodder and Stoughton.

9 | 'I listened carefully to the way children were spoken to' – equality and the under-threes!

Fiona Fogarty

Educational establishments and other pre-school day care settings can sometimes seem like their own little worlds. Many aspects of the physical environment are shared, modified and experienced in common. Activities are set up and timings agreed. Organizational and logistical decisions may be debated and then implemented. Routines develop around the deployment of resources and it is often a challenge from outside – perhaps new government guidelines or a new manager – which is the catalyst for major change.

Equal opportunities policies and their implementation in practice stem from the interface between what has been taken for granted in a particular institutional setting and reflections on the world outside with its diverse cultural influences. Thinking about equal opportunities is often not easy; it is never easy to jolt oneself into questioning the ideas and preconceptions that seem to have 'worked' for ourselves and/or our immediate ancestors.

This chapter therefore does not offer a smooth argument or picture as to what equal opportunities should look like for the under-threes. Rather it presents some fragmented glimpses into certain issues which I believe are important – from a brief look at current changing definitions of 'equal opportunities' to very specific examples in practice. I hope that those adults who wish to make a considered approach to the kinds of experiences and environments shared with children under 3, whatever their relationship with those children, may find my reflections stimulating.

I work as a teacher in a community school, where children arrive in the nursery at the age of 3 with very different previous experiences from my own young daughter. They may speak a different language at home, or have different cultural backgrounds and expectations of school. I believe, though, that there are kinds of experiences for the under-threes which I consider to be the right of every child. In order to explain, it is important that I highlight some of the principles which I consider to be important in the provision of early experiences and review some of the contributions which have helped to formulate my own views.

The school in which I work has a carefully considered equal opportunities policy which is owned and implemented by all members of staff who work with children between the ages of 3 and 11. I have worked with all primary school age groups but it was not until I had to consider the kind of 'educare' experience I wanted for my own daughter Evie (now 2 years, 1 month) that I had to define my own views on equal opportunities and the under-threes.

How are equal opportunities defined?

Smedley (1996) considers that the terms we choose to use in educational discourse are significant and not static. She uses the terms 'equality' and 'equity' to emphasize justice and fairness, rather than sameness:

> 'Equality of opportunity' might be a more familiar term, but sometimes familiarity can be a disadvantage; the term can tend to trip off the tongue all too easily. Equality of opportunity may also seem like rather a tired term – familiarity can breed contempt, at best indifference, or feed into a backlash that claims that equality of opportunity is no longer an issue.
>
> (Smedley 1996: 104)

The Children Act (1989) states that 'Children have a right to an environment which facilitates their development' (DoH 1991: 6, s. 28) and considers children's rights in terms of their developing sense of identity, including the right to individuality, respect, dignity and freedom from discrimination such as racism and sexism. These matters are examined by both Helen Moylett and Brenda Griffin in Chapters 1 and 2.

In describing the Children Act, Siraj-Blatchford (1992: 110) considers it 'an exciting move towards equality' and the 'first piece of legislation on the care of children which refers specifically to catering for children's racial, religious, cultural and linguistic backgrounds'. But as Smedley (1996) observes, legislation needs to be brought to life by people.

The people in the life of a child below the age of 3, whether parent or carer, nursery nurse or teacher, childminder or family friend, exert a powerful influence on the developing self. Gender role studies indicate that from birth, children learn the values of the social groups in which they live (Lloyd 1987). Drummond *et al.* (1992: 9) recommend that 'educarers' ask themselves why they do what they do, in order to uncover the value positions they represent. They argue that the principle of 'the loving use of power' applies here as throughout early childhood and is non-negotiable.

Any definition of 'equality of opportunity' must be contrasted with an understanding of what is meant by 'inequality'. By definition this refers to a lack of access to opportunity. The built-in assumption is that access is possible via an equal opportunities policy – but that is dependent ultimately on the people responsible for its implementation.

We are back to people again! The focus of this book is upon the adults who work with, care about, are responsible for children under 3 and on whom the responsibility for the equality of opportunity rests.

An equal opportunities policy must take into account the difference in power between various people. Sadly, often a child is not taken seriously; they are regarded as an appendage rather than respected and accepted as having their own, independent voice. In examining 'multiple perspectives on equality' in relation to early childhood programmes in the United States, Katz (1995) argues that the child's objective experience is determined by effects over time. She suggests that adults should ask on behalf of the child, 'What does it feel like to be a child in this environment day after day?' This is a question that I found myself attempting to answer quite often as a teacher, when evaluating the kinds of curriculum experiences which I offered to my children. When it came to deciding on the kind of childcare I wanted for my own very young baby, I then began to ask 'What kind of environment do I want her to experience day after day?' and 'How do I want her to feel?'

My own experience as a teacher has taught me that the development of positive, respectful and supportive relations between staff and parents who share a background of culture, language and ethnicity is relatively easy, but the development of such relationships between 'educarers' and parents of diverse backgrounds requires insight, judgement and professionalism, and depends on personal values. These were the attributes I would have in mind as I made important decisions about the care and education of my own child.

Although most of my professional experience has been with children over the age of 3, I consider that it is this interaction with children, parents and the wider community that has helped to shape my views and expectations about the under-threes. It is therefore important that I now trace my development and share some of these experiences.

My own experience as a teacher

For the past 11 years I have taught in a large inner-city community primary school. I have worked as class teacher, support teacher, unit coordinator and as acting deputy. Although I have worked with pupils from every age range I am now based solely in reception, supporting bilingual pupils in my capacity as LEAP (Section 11 Language for Education Access Project) coordinator.

For a time I was the curriculum access coordinator. My job involved helping class teachers, at planning stage, by suggesting strategies that would enable as many pupils as possible to benefit from the curriculum on offer to them. I also devised and implemented activities for specific groups of pupils who, for whatever reason, were disenfranchised from the curriculum and were in need of some extra support and encouragement. They might be pupils with behavioural or learning difficulties, but for the majority of pupils at the school the pressing need was to have the curriculum adapted to suit the requirements of children learning English as an additional language. To support good acquisition and a fair opportunity to succeed we needed to contextualize much of the curriculum and include many first-hand experiences. We had to group with sensitivity, allowing beginners to work with more fluent pupils. Generally we needed to have a sound, structured approach to language teaching.

There are many ways of addressing those needs (and indeed the school did not restrict itself to one approach), but in developing structured play from nursery through to top juniors I felt the school's response was particularly creative and successful.

To us, creating a structured play area meant building and researching an area in such a way that it supported the skills and concepts identified in our planning. For instance, to support work on media studies with junior pupils we built a TV studio. Here was the potential to support many areas of the curriculum through costume design and make-up to light filters and camera angles. Pupils were able to plan, prepare and video short programmes and later review their efforts.

Such a tangible and practical approach proved a very successful means of offering additional access to the curriculum. As the coordinator responsible I became increasingly involved in structured play; I have spent the last 11 years principally engaged in planning, building, teaching in and monitoring play areas throughout the school.

In building a structured play area you have the opportunity to create a 'little world' within the real world, and as such you can make it as perfect as you like. Certainly as a school we were not slow to use it to reflect those values we wished to promote. For instance, pupils may have come from homes where all the cooking and cleaning was done by women while men spent long hours out at work. But in our home corners, at least, they would see images of men cooking and of women engaged in a variety of occupations. Even though our own school could not boast many non-white role models, our displays reflected a whole world of different people busily leading their successful lives.

The play areas were arranged to offer a safe, consistent place in which to confront and challenge issues of racism and sexism. In the railway station structured play area it was easy to challenge the boy who said that girls couldn't drive trains. He was shown the prominently displayed photograph of a woman train driver and the duty roster where lots of girls had signed up to be the driver. He was also asked to explain why he thought that. At the end of the day he was helped to enjoy the 'railway game', not only when he was the driver but also when a girl was the driver and he was a ticket collector or passenger. The incentive in structured play to negotiate, resolve problems and get on with the game should not be underestimated as a force for motivation.

However, issues arising were not always as predictable as that. On one occasion we became concerned that some Year 1 and 2 boys were not using the home corner that was itself part of a larger structured play area, the airport. It seemed very likely that the boys were shunning the mere domestic for the glamour of the cockpit. We decided to talk to them and monitor proceedings.

To our surprise it turned out that, far from not wanting to use the home corner, they were being turned out and ridiculed by a group of dominant Year 2 girls. It was the girls who were using gender stereotypes to force the boys out so they could play with babies and have parties with the play food. We responded by discussing the problem and by encouraging the girls to explore other parts of the structured play area and see themselves in roles of pilot, customs officer or air traffic controller. We also timetabled opportunities for the boys to use the house, which they did with gusto.

The school promoted the use of structured play areas because they seemed to offer so many opportunities:

- they involved all pupils and allowed them to join in at their own level. Children were more concerned with organizing themselves into a successful 'game' than judging or rejecting others. Pupils new to English or with special educational needs could find a lot they felt comfortable with;
- pupils needed to negotiate and cooperate in order to succeed;
- they had to be responsible for their behaviour and resources.

The whole experience was one which boosted their personal esteem and the pleasure of it coloured their perception of school. Previously enjoyed structured play areas always feature in fond reminiscence when I meet past pupils. Structured play was one important element in a conscientious school's attempt to create equal opportunities for its pupils. We couldn't hope to change the world but at least our pupils would leave us with fired imaginations, high expectations and the skills and strategies to tackle problems that confronted them.

My daughter and myself

After so much experience of the hard work and invention required in cultivating an atmosphere conducive to the promotion of equal opportunities I had clear ideas about the out-of-home provision I wanted for my own daughter.

She was 7 months old and I needed to find part-time provision for her. The local authority furnished me with the usual lists and I set about my task with enthusiasm.

- I wanted my little girl to be cared for in a comfortable and friendly place.
- I hoped that she would have the opportunity to mix, right from the start, with boys and girls from other races and that she would have the same chance as any of them to join in what was on offer.
- I did not want race, gender or disability issues to be thrust at my daughter but I hoped that her carers would be prepared so that when issues did arise they would be handled with sensitivity and clear objectives.

Siraj-Blatchford (1996) considers that early years educators are often inexperienced and lack the knowledge and understanding of how children become biased and how to deal with these matters. Walkerdine (1987) found that they often display a profound sense of inadequacy when faced with sexism and racism from children. Yet it is only natural that young children will learn the behaviours and adopt the responses and attitudes to which they are systematically exposed. I wanted my child to be cared for by adults who were open, honest, fair minded, non-judgemental and who had considered carefully their responses to the above issues.

I visited childminders and was impressed. One in particular handled me, as an anxious parent, very well. She was very businesslike about practical arrangements and invited me and my daughter to her home so that we could talk and I could see her handle my baby. I do not know quite what I expected, but she surprised me by quickly turning the conversation around to her values with regard to handling children. Nothing she actually said perturbed me but I became suddenly overwhelmed by the realization that I would be handing over my beautiful, new, open-minded baby and exposing her to a stranger's beliefs, opinions and prejudices. Even among close friends it is rare to find someone whose values mirror your own precisely. The alarming prospect of my own child voicing some ugly sentiment, completely beyond my influence, was too much.

I decided instead to investigate nurseries in my area in the hope that an institution was

- more likely to have trained staff who would have received guidance in dealing with equal opportunity issues and behaviour management;
- more likely to have written policies and guidelines that I could consult;
- unlikely to tolerate behaviour from staff and children that contravened such policies.

I also hoped that by being handled by more than one adult my little girl would be less likely to come under the strong influence of one person's attitudes and behaviour. It is interesting that my decision contrasts with that of Helen Moylett (Chapter 1), who chose a childminder rather than a nursery for her young son.

Most of the nurseries I visited were quick to display a variety of resources and to assure me that both sexes had equal access to them. Many had structured play areas but sadly few seemed to have approached them with lively invention, nor did they have the same high expectations of their value as I did.

I saw few images of black or Asian people on display, few black dolls and, sadly, little racial mix within the nursery staff or children. The make-up was nearly 100 per cent white.

Visiting the nurseries, however, I became aware that I was less concerned with pictures and resources and more anxious to pick up on the prevailing attitude towards the children. I listened carefully to the way the children were spoken to. I wanted to see children being treated with respect, and attention being paid to their ideas.

I was hopeful that my daughter would be encouraged to develop confidence and self-esteem so that when faced by any new experience she wouldn't feel automatically excluded for any irrelevant reason, such as her gender. I also hoped she would not go unchallenged when she, herself, voiced an unreasonable prejudice.

I knew that having the opportunity to play with the 'right' toys and see the 'right' images would shape my daughter's outlook, but I believed the attitudes of the adults around her would have a more immediate and profound effect on her character.

It must be said that there was a great deal more to the process of giving over my tiny baby to the care of others than can be encapsulated in a set of principles or opinions. I had very strong and mixed emotions. Would a carer become a rival influence? Would anybody be as kind, attentive and gentle to her as I would want? Would somebody notice her every change of mood and need?

Now that I can look back and reflect on the 18 months' nursery care my child has received, I can see that my maternal feelings and my more intellectual opinions were leading me in the same directions. I believe that unless a child is valued and made to feel of worth they are unlikely to value and respect others. That was what mattered most to me.

Ironically I might have saved myself all the effort and anxiety because, childcare provision being what it is, there was only one nursery that could offer me a place for my little girl. I was fortunate with the nursery . . . but it came down to luck in the end.

As I prepared to leave my baby there, I was overwhelmed by concerns – would she sleep? eat? cry? Would she settle? It is with consummate relief I can report she did.

References

Department of Health [DoH] (1991) *The Children Act 1989 Guidance and Regulations Vol. 2: Family Support, Day Care and Educational Provision for Young Children.* London: HMSO.

Drummond, M. J., Rouse, D. and Pugh, G. (1992) *Making Assessment Work: Values and Principles in Assessing Young Children's Learning.* London: NES Arnold in association with the National Children's Bureau.

Katz, L. (1995) Multiple perspectives on quality. Paper presented at BAECE Conference, London, September.

Lloyd, B. (1987) Social representations of gender, in J. Bruner and H. Haste (eds) *Making Sense.* London: Methuen.

Siraj-Blatchford, I. (1992) Why understanding cultural differences is not enough, in G. Pugh (ed.) *Contemporary Issues in the Early Years.* London: Paul Chapman in association with the National Children's Bureau.

Siraj-Blatchford, I. (1996) Language, culture and difference: challenging inequality and promoting respect, in C. Nutbrown (ed.) *Respectful Educators – Capable Learners: Children's Rights and Early Education.* London: Paul Chapman.

Smedley, S. (1996) Looking for equality and equity, in R. Robson and S. Smedley *Education in Early Childhood.* London: David Fulton Publishers in association with the Roehampton Institute.

Walkerdine, V. (1987) Sex, power and pedagogy, in M. Arnot and G. Weiner (eds) *Gender and the Politics of Schooling.* London: Unwin Hyman.

Concluding thoughts – drawing the threads together

Helen Moylett

Child

Your clear eye is the one absolutely beautiful thing
I want to fill it with color and ducks,
The zoo of the new

Whose names you meditate –
April snowdrop, Indian pipe,
Little

Stalk without wrinkle,
Pool in which images
Should be grand and classical

Not this troublous
Wringing of hands, this dark
Ceiling without a star.

Sylvia Plath (1963)

This poem was written only a few days before Sylvia Plath took her own life, presumably able only to see the 'dark ceiling'. It may therefore seem an odd choice to use in concluding a book full of hope and optimism for the future. However, it seems to say so much about the curiosity and wonder of childhood and the way in which its essential purity and joy can be so easily and quickly threatened by adults who cannot, for whatever reason, share the wonder or see the stars.

The contributors to this book can certainly see those stars. Just as in *Working with the Under-threes: training and professional development*, there is a diversity of views represented here but there are also some powerful strands that link all the writers. What comes over very strongly is a deep curiosity and a real commitment to learning – not just children's learning but their own as well. Each writer talks about what they have learned from the children as part of the discussion about what the children have learned. We see adult and child learners going along an exciting road hand in hand. Sometimes there are bits of the road that the adult knows well and can help the child over, sometimes the child finds new ways to travel or sees the road differently and responds differently from the adult. Consider the determined

Oliver described by Hilary Renowden in Chapter 6 who regularly makes his way out of the beautifully appointed baby unit, to where he really wants to be – with the older children and their resources. The adults do not respond by putting him back in his ghetto but have learned from his behaviour and are interested both in what he does and in what his actions mean. Think about the children in Ruth Holland's nursery described in Chapter 7 who, thanks to her curiosity about how children respond to heuristic play opportunities, have demonstrated their need to explore materials without being pressured into adult-orientated products. She and the staff have not concluded that the children are wrong to behave in the ways they do, but have seen this as a valuable learning experience for them which has led to changed provision for the children.

These are just two examples, from the many in the book, of children and adults learning from and about one another. The majority of children mentioned in this book are fortunate people. They are having their worth confirmed in all sorts of ways and becoming confident, curious makers of meaning and shapers of context. We see Kathleen in Chapter 5 being given space to evolve her own ways of using a nursery rhyme. Connor in Chapter 1 is able to interrupt adult conversation effectively, and then there are all those children discussed by Caroline Barratt-Pugh in Chapters 3 and 4 who believe in their own ability to make spoken and written language work for them. The adults they work with are open to the messages they are given by these very young learners and respect them as people. The effect of this sort of openness to children and their vulnerability is described beautifully in the last lines of Elizabeth Jennings's (1986) poem 'Losing and Finding':

> You took me out of time, rubbed off on me
> What it feels like to care without restriction,
> To trust and never think of a betrayal.

Jennings is talking about interaction with a 6-year-old who barges unceremoniously and needily into adult isolation, but the age of the child is largely irrelevant. She pinpoints the way in which those who listen to children may begin to have access to a world which they have forgotten or long since repressed: a world which is uninhibited, full of strong emotions and unsullied by cynicism. To engage with these children is to accept the robust and curious accounts of the world they offer, not to dismiss them as childish fancies. The children in this book are successful both intellectually and socially because adults have bothered to listen and think about both their intellectual and social development. These children are all able to use language to communicate effectively both with each other and with adults, and they clearly see purpose in so doing. Unfortunately, because it is such a contrast with the majority, Brenda Griffin's description at the beginning of Chapter 2 of sad little disempowered Alex will, I am sure, remain with many readers.

Alex reminded me of so many children and indirectly caused me to re-read Riseborough (1993). This may seem a million miles from the world of the under-threes, dealing as it does with 'the YTS boys' of the self-styled 'Gobbo Barmy Harmy'. Riseborough provides a vivid insight into the ways in which these lads conduct themselves in the world. It is both shocking and amusing and contains many issues to ponder, but it is essentially a story of oppression. Unlike the children in this book, an intellectual and social divide has obviously widened between these lads and much of the rest of society. They behave in ways which are socially outrageous, and in their deviance have withdrawn into a sort of clan which admits of no diversity from their own violent, racist, sexist and disablist norms. Although they doubtless have been, and still are, the victims of oppression they have built a world with meaning for themselves on the margins. The powerful link for me between these lads and little Alex is the potentially cumulative effect of failure. We know that the early years are when people learn the most – how tragic that for too many they learn that they do not count; that their version of events is never listened to.

How often do sad little Alexes turn into big, violent, anti-social yobs? Their commonality is their failure – and ours as adults – to value their versions of the world then, now or in the future.

Of course there are all sorts of equal opportunity issues involved here. Allatt (1993), in her study of three middle-class families, notes how successful they are in handing on the necessary cultural capital for educational, social and career success. Tizard and Hughes (1984) indicate the ways in which stereotyped views of working-class families can be maintained because middle-class parents appear to be able to pass on this cultural capital in ways which affect their children's ability to relate more 'successfully' to the middle-class world of nursery than working-class children. The opening paragraph of Siraj-Blatchford (1994) highlights the effect of racism from and towards very young children – the sort of situation Fiona Fogarty talks about wanting to avoid in Chapter 9. Much interesting work has been done about the ways in which gender issues may affect girls' and boys' performance in the early years and the ways educarers relate to them (see for example Walkerdine 1981; Browne and France 1986).

However, while not wishing to deny the very powerful effect these, and other, forms of discrimination have on all our lives, it must be remembered that, although children are not a minority group (although many belong to various minority groups) they are certainly discriminated against just by virtue of being children. Even those who are white, male, middle class, able bodied and heterosexual are subject to adult power and prejudice. Those of us who live in Britain still live in a society which has not moved all that far from Victorian notions of children being seen and not heard although, as Brenda Griffin points out in Chapter 2, there are benefits in seeing ourselves as world citizens and being open to other options. The writers of this book are distinguished by their ability to hear and have respect for the people with whom they work. They provide powerful role models for these young people who are learning about how to be socially and intellectually skilled. As Siraj-Blatchford (1996: 24) says, 'children can only learn to be tolerant, challenge unfair generalizations and learn inclusiveness and positive regard for difference if they see the adults around them do the same'.

All the writers discuss life experiences that have caused them to think about children in respectful ways and to act in the ways they describe in their chapters. Fiona Fogarty cites her teaching experience and commitment to structured play, Hilary Renowden talks about her disillusionment with the state system and the power that running her own private nursery has given her to implement her ideas about creativity. Like Brenda Griffin, she has been influenced by her positive experiences of Scandinavian childcare settings. Brenda Kyle emphasizes the power her headship gave her to work with the family – rather than the child alone – in helping people (including other teachers) see children, whatever their special needs, as people in their own right. Caroline Barratt-Pugh talks about 25 years of curiosity developing into systematic research about how children become language users. Julia Gillen's work in linguistics has been both prompted and enriched by her own children's experiences.

All the adults writing, or written about, in this book are challenging the status quo from positions of experience and knowledge. They are saying some valuable things about our youngest children – our collective future – which we wanted to share with a wider audience. We feel that educarers working with all age groups might find some of these accounts of children and adults working together illuminating. We hope the books will help those working with our youngest citizens to value their own contributions and to remain inspired star gazers!

References

Allatt, P. (1993) Becoming privileged, in I. Bates and G. Riseborough (eds) *Youth and Inequality*. Buckingham: Open University Press.

Browne, N. and France, P. (eds) (1986) *Untying the Apron Strings*. Milton Keynes: Open University Press.

Jennings, E. (1986) 'Losing and Finding', in *Collected Poems*. Manchester: Carcanet.

Plath, S. (1963) 'Child', in *Collected Poems* (ed. T. Hughes). London: Faber.

Riseborough, G. (1993) GBH – the Gobbo Barmy Harmy, in I. Bates and G. Riseborough (eds) *Youth and Inequality*. Buckingham: Open University Press.

Siraj-Blatchford, I. (1994) *The Early Years, Laying the Foundations for Racial Equality*. Stoke on Trent: Trentham Books.

Siraj-Blatchford, I. (1996) Language, culture and difference: challenging inequality and promoting respect, in C. Nutbrown (ed.) *Children's Rights and Early Education*. London: Paul Chapman Publishing.

Tizard, B. and Hughes, M. (1984) *Young Children Learning*. London: Fontana.

Walkerdine, V. (1981) Sex, power and pedagogy, in V. Walkerdine *Schoolgirl Fictions*. London: Verso.

Index

QUALITY EDUCATION IN THE EARLY YEARS

Lesley Abbott and Rosemary Rodger (eds)

Lesley Abbott and her team of contributors identify and explore high quality work (and what shapes it) in early years education. They show us children and adults variously working and playing, talking and communicating, learning and laughing, caring and sharing in a rich tapestry of case studies which highlight quality experiences and interactions. Every chapter is based around a particular case study, each one tackling a different issue: the curriculum, play, assessment, roles and relationships, special needs, partnerships with parents, and equal opportunities.

All the writers work together in early years education on a day-to-day basis enabling them to pool their different expertise to create a balanced but challenging approach. They give inspiring examples of, and outline underlying principles for, quality work and ask important questions of all those involved in the education and care of young children.

Contents
Introduction: The search for quality in the early years – A quality curriculum in the early years: Raising some questions – 'Play is fun, but it's hard work too': The search for quality play in the early years – 'Why involve me?' Encouraging children and their parents to participate in the assessment process – 'It's nice here now': Managing young children's behaviour – 'She'll have a go at anything': Towards an equal opportunities policy – 'We only speak English here, don't we?' Supporting language development in a multilingual context – 'People matter': The role of adults in providing a quality learning environment for the early years – 'You feel like you belong': Establishing partnerships between parents and educators – 'Look at me – I'm only two': Educare for the under threes: The importance of early experience – Looking to the future: Concluding comments – Bibliography – Index.

Contributors
Lesley Abbott, Janet Ackers, Janice Adams, Caroline Barratt-Pugh, Brenda Griffin, Chris Marsh, Sylvia Phillips, Rosemary Rodger, Helen Strahan.

224pp   0 335 19230 0 (Paperback)   0 335 19231 9 (Hardback)

STARTING FROM THE CHILD?

TEACHING AND LEARNING FROM 4 TO 8

Julie Fisher

Early years practitioners currently face a number of dilemmas when planning an education for young children. The imposition of an external curriculum seems to work in opposition to the principles of planning experiences which start from the child. Does this mean that the notion of a curriculum centred on the needs and interests of children is now more rhetoric than reality?

In a practical and realistic way *Starting from the Child?* examines a range of theories about young children as learners and the implications of these theories for classroom practice. Julie Fisher acknowledges the competence of young children when they arrive at school, the importance of building on their early successes and the critical role of adults who understand the individual and idiosyncratic ways of young learners. The book addresses the key issues of planning and assessment, explores the place of talk and play in the classroom and examines the role of the teacher in keeping a balance between the demands of the curriculum and the learning needs of the child.

This is essential reading, not only for early years practitioners, but for all those who manage and make decisions about early learning.

Contents
Competent young learners – Conversations and observations – Planning for learning – The role of the teacher – Encouraging independence – Collaboration and cooperation – The place of play – The negotiated classroom – Planning, doing and reviewing – Evaluation and assessment – References – Index.

192pp   0 335 19556 3 (Paperback)   0 335 19557 1 (Hardback)

THE EXCELLENCE OF PLAY

Janet R. Moyles (ed.)

Child: When I play with my friends we have lots of fun . . . do lots of things . . . think about stuff . . . and . . . well . . .

Adult: Do you think you learn anything?

Child: Heaps and heaps – not like about sums and books and things . . . um . . . like . . . well . . . like *real* things.

Anyone who has observed play for any length of time will recognize that, for young children, play is a tool for learning. Professionals who understand, acknowledge, and appreciate this can, through provision, interaction and intervention in children's play, ensure progression, differentiation and relevance in the curriculum.

The Excellence of Play gathers together authoritative contributors to provide a wide-ranging and key source text reflecting both up-to-date research and current classroom practice. It tackles how we conceptualize play, how we 'place' it in the classroom, how we relate it to the curriculum, and how we evaluate its role in learning in the early years. It will stimulate and inform debate through its powerful argument that 'a curriculum which sanctions and utilizes play is more likely to provide well-balanced citizens of the future as well as happier children in the present'.

Contents

Introduction – Part 1: The culture of play and childhood – Play and the uses of play – Play in different cultures and different childhoods – Sex-differentiated play experiences and children's choices – Play, the playground and the culture of childhood – Part 2: Play, schooling and responsibilities – Play and legislated curriculum. Back to basics: an alternative view – 'Play is ace!' Developing play in schools and classrooms – Fantasy play: a case for adult intervention – Making play work in the classroom – Part 3: Play and the early years curriculum – Play, literacy and the role of the teacher – Experiential learning in play and art – Bulbs, buzzers and batteries: play and science – Mathematics and play – Part 4: Assessing and evaluating play – Evaluating and improving the quality of play – Observing play in early childhood – Play, the universe and everything! – Afterword – References – Index.

Contributors

Lesley Abbott, Angela Anning, Tony Bertram, David Brown, Tina Bruce, Audrey Curtis, Rose Griffiths, Nigel Hall, Peter Heaslip, Jane Hislam, Victoria Hurst, Neil Kitson, Janet R. Moyles, Christine Pascal, Roy Prentice, Jeni Riley, Jane Savage, Peter K. Smith.

240pp   0 335 19068 5 (Paperback)